More Praise for *Take Charge o*

"This book offers you the keys to ignite your personal power."
—**from the foreword by Jim Kouzes, coauthor of the bestselling *The Leadership Challenge***

"I've seen the key practices in *Take Charge of Your Talent* work with hundreds of people—from frontline employees to CEO. Read it and help your career and your organization thrive."
—**Frank Benest, Senior Advisor for Next Generation Initiatives, International City/County Management Association**

"I've long been aware that even the best of our company-sponsored talent development programs reach only a select few, leaving tremendous potential in the organization untapped. This powerful, persuasive book effectively supplies the tools for all employees to gain a fresh perspective, articulate aspirations, and recognize opportunities while confronting concerns and obstacles to gain results."
—**Ursula Kiel-Dixon, Special Projects Manager, Corporate Center Human Resources, ThyssenKrupp AG**

"In the new era of free agents, this book provides exactly what both individuals and organizations are looking for. Don and Jay have delivered a proven and easy-to-understand process for the development of an organization's most precious resource, its talent pool. In so doing, they inspire more job satisfaction and greater career fulfillment."
—**John Steinhart, Silicon Valley human resources consultant and former Director, Sloan Executive Program, Stanford Graduate School of Business**

"The heart of this book is a profound but easy-to-learn approach to becoming a 'generous listener.' Using the transformational power of this mindful practice, Maruska and Perry expertly guide the reader in a step-by-step process for recognizing, catalyzing, and optimizing your talent while helping others discover and express theirs. Highly recommended."
—**Michael J. Gelb, author of *How to Think Like Leonardo da Vinci* and coauthor of *Brain Power***

"All too often, I hear promising young talents speak of being 'lucky' in their careers. I hate that. You make your own luck by knowing your strengths, embracing risk, and leading change. This book has the keys to unlocking what makes you thrive so that you can give voice to your ambition with authenticity and purpose."

—Denny Marie Post, Senior Vice President and Chief Marketing Officer, Red Robin International

"The world is filled with people who never realize their potential, many of whom never even realize they have unfulfilled potential. *Take Charge of Your Talent* provides an effective game plan for helping people move toward their hopes for what they might become."

—Jim Thompson, founder, Positive Coaching Alliance, and author of *Elevating Your Game*

"This practical book, filled with detailed coaching and useful exercises, reflects the extensive experience of the authors in coaching executives. This book will help you clarify, enhance, and find ways to apply your talents."

—Jim Clawson, Johnson & Higgins Professor of Business Administration, Darden School of Business, University of Virginia

"*Take Charge of Your Talent* is a positive and refreshing approach to talent development. The Take Charge methodology offers techniques on how to own and grow your career while supporting the personal and professional development of your colleagues—creating a win-win for all!"

—Renée Robertson, former Director of Talent Development, Verizon

"The powerful tools offered in this book provide the only real security we have in today's job market—the ability to take control and fully realize one's talent."

—Dawn Legg, Construction Liaison, Topaz Solar Farms, First Solar

"The gem of *Take Charge of Your Talent* is that it reinforces the (often lost) reality that there are opportunities at any time, in any business climate. It is the prospect for meaningful productivity using your unique talents that lights the fire."

—John C. Summer, Director of Business Development, Taylor Frigon Capital Management LLC

"I had the opportunity to experience the Talent Catalyst Conversation with many of my HR colleagues, and it was amazing to see how following the process led to igniting possibilities for the participants. I hope Maruska and Perry realize their vision of 20 million people in 20 countries having these keys to take charge of their talent by the year 2020!"

—Donna Vaillancourt, President, County Personnel Administrators Association of California

TAKE CHARGE OF YOUR TALENT

TAKE CHARGE OF YOUR TALENT

Three Keys to Thriving in Your Career, Organization, and Life

Don Maruska & Jay Perry

BK

Berrett–Koehler Publishers, Inc.
San Francisco
a BK Life book

Berrett-Koehler Publishers, Inc.
235 Montgomery Street, Suite 650, San Francisco, CA 94104-2916
Tel: (415) 288-0260 • Fax: (415) 362-2512 • www.bkconnection.com

ORDERING INFORMATION

QUANTITY SALES. Special discounts are available on quantity purchases by corporations, associations, and others. For details, contact the "Special Sales Department" at the Berrett-Koehler address above.

INDIVIDUAL SALES. Berrett-Koehler publications are available through most bookstores. They can also be ordered directly from Berrett-Koehler: Tel: (800) 929-2929; Fax: (802) 864-7626; www.bkconnection.com

ORDERS FOR COLLEGE TEXTBOOK/COURSE ADOPTION USE. Please contact Berrett-Koehler: Tel: (800) 929-2929; Fax: (802) 864-7626.

ORDERS BY U.S. TRADE BOOKSTORES AND WHOLESALERS. Please contact Ingram Publisher Services, Tel: (800) 509-4887; Fax: (800) 838-1149; E-mail: customer.service @ingrampublisherservices.com; or visit www.ingrampublisherservices.com/Ordering for details about electronic ordering.

Berrett-Koehler and the BK logo are registered trademarks of Berrett-Koehler Publishers, Inc.

Printed in the United States of America

Berrett-Koehler books are printed on long-lasting acid-free paper. When it is available, we choose paper that has been manufactured by environmentally responsible processes. These may include using trees grown in sustainable forests, incorporating recycled paper, minimizing chlorine in bleaching, or recycling the energy produced at the paper mill.

LIBRARY OF CONGRESS CATALOGING-IN-PUBLICATION DATA

Maruska, Don.
Take charge of your talent : three keys to thriving in your career, organization, and life / Don Maruska and Jay Perry.
    p. cm.
Includes bibliographical references and index.
ISBN 978-1-60994-723-1 (pbk.)
1. Career development. 2. Success in business. 3. Success. I. Perry, Jay. II. Title.
HF5381.M374 2013
650.1—dc23

2012035413

FIRST EDITION

17 16 15 14 13 12   10 9 8 7 6 5 4 3 2 1

Cover design by PemaStudio. Project management and interior design by VJBScribe. Copyediting by Elissa Rabellino. Proofreading by Don Roberts. Index by George Draffan. Interior photos: Don Maruska, Bella Castle Photography; Jay Perry, Jen Fariello Photography.

We dedicate this book to our parents, spouses, and children, and to the many teachers who nurtured us and encouraged us to take charge of our talent.

CONTENTS

RESOURCES

FOREWORD:
THREE TRUTHS ABOUT TALENT

Jim Kouzes

As I was reading *Take Charge of Your Talent*, I was reminded of something Melissa Poe Hood said about the work she had done in leading Kids For a Clean Environment (Kids F.A.C.E.), an organization she started when she was a fourth grader in Nashville, Tennessee. In accepting the Women of Distinction Award from the American Association of University Women and the National Association of Student Personnel Administrators twenty years after her initial efforts, Melissa offered this advice:

> *Change does not begin with someone else. Change begins in your own backyard, no matter your age or your size. I had no idea that one simple action could change my life so much. Most journeys start this way, with simple motivation and a choice to do something or not. You never know where one step will take you, and you never know where the next one will lead. The difference with being a leader is that you take the step; you take the journey. The greatest obstacle you will ever encounter is yourself. Just like Dorothy never knew that she always had the ticket home, the Scarecrow always had a brain, the Tin Man always had a compassionate heart, even the Cowardly Lion had courage. Everything you need to be a successful leader you already have: your intelligence to see an issue and a way to fix*

*it, your heart to stay motivated, and your courage not to give up.
You can't look for the man behind the curtain to solve your
concerns. Everything you need you already have. It's all about
taking the first step.*[1]

Melissa's remarks go straight to the heart of what this
marvelous little book is all about. She affirms—and is living
proof—that each and every person has the power to make
extraordinary things happen in his or her life. What is required,
however, as Melissa implies, is that each and every person also
take personal responsibility for using that power.

And that's why this book by Don Maruska and Jay Perry is
so important and so useful. They give us the methodology and
the tools to bring out what is already there. This book offers you
the keys to ignite your personal power.

Don and Jay talk about three keys—Power Up Your Talent
Story, Accelerate through Obstacles, and Multiply the Payoffs for
Yourself and Others. Each of these, I submit, is based on three
fundamental truths about what it takes to perform at your personal best.

The first truth is that *you make a difference*. It is the most fundamental truth of all. Before you can take charge of your talent,
you have to believe that you can have a positive impact on your
own life and career. You have to believe that you have it in you
to improve what you do and how you do it.

When Don and Jay talk about how you are the hero of your
own story and you can reclaim the power of your story, they
are saying, at least to me, that you have to believe your future is
in your hands and not controlled by somebody or something
else—a manager, a parent, your genes, the rotten hand that you
were dealt. This doesn't mean that context doesn't matter, that
you can deny the laws of nature, or that other people don't also
have something to say about what you do. What it does mean is
that the hand turning the key is yours and not someone else's.

That's where it all begins. You have to believe that you can make a difference. You have to believe that your life counts for something. You have to believe in yourself. If you don't, you won't even try. It begins with you.

The second truth is that *challenge is the crucible of greatness.* Barry Posner and I have been studying what leaders do when they're at their personal best for over thirty years, and in every single case there is some element of challenge, difficulty, adversity, and uncertainty. There has never been a single case in the thousands we've analyzed in which someone did his or her best when keeping things exactly the way they were. Doing one's best is never about doing the same thing just a little bit better. It's always about doing different things, new things, and innovative things extraordinarily better. Whatever the function people are in, giving an Olympic-level performance is always about pushing the limits, exceeding prior records, dealing with adversity, and learning from failure.

Great achievements just don't happen when you keep things the same. Change invariably involves challenge, and challenge tests you. It introduces you to yourself. It brings you face-to-face with your level of commitment, your grittiness, and your values. It reveals your mind-set about change.

In *Take Charge of Your Talent*, Don and Jay help you learn how to master frustration, overcome discouragement, and get past self-imposed or externally imposed limits. They talk to you about, for example, how to make your hopes visible, how to turn concerns into energizers, how to craft an inspirational personal story, and, my favorite, how to get your *but* out of the way. They offer checklists and resources that help you to take charge.

The third truth that's evident in this book is that *you can't do it alone.* No one ever got anything extraordinary done without the talent and support of others. You can graduate at the top of the class from the best schools in the world; reason circles around your brightest peers; solve technical problems with wizardlike powers; and have the relevant situational, functional, and industry experience, and *still* be more likely to fail than to succeed—unless you also possess the requisite personal and social skills. The mandate is very clear. You have to learn how to work well with others in order to become your best.

While you are the hero of this book and the central character in your story, you are definitely not the only actor. This is evident in the third key—Multiply the Payoffs for Yourself and Others—but it's also a message that's woven through the other two keys to taking charge of your talent. Throughout this book there is a requirement that you work with a Talent Catalyst to implement the tested process that Don and Jay have designed. That person could be a coworker, friend, family member, or acquaintance, but this is a process you can't do alone. You have to do it with someone else. Don and Jay even offer you a handy sample of how a Talent Catalyst Conversation goes so that you can see how it's been done before.

Studies of top performers strongly suggest that you have to have a supportive environment in order to develop expertise. A supportive family is very common in the stories of world-class performers. Supportive colleagues at work are critical. Leadership can't grow in a culture that isn't supportive of continuing development. You need to surround yourself with people who are going to offer you encouraging words when you try something new, understanding and patience when you fail, and helpful suggestions as you try to learn from mistakes.

Don and Jay ask you to go one step further. They ask you to apply the lessons you learn toward the goal of serving others. This reminds me of the hand-carved wooden plaque my wife and I saw nailed to the side of a store in the historic mountain town of Truckee, California. It was dedicated to the memory of Joseph Ignatius Firpo, and it read: "What we have done for ourselves dies with us. What we have done for others remains, and is immortal." The legacy you leave lives on, not in what you have done for yourself; when you go, it goes with you. But what you do to teach others, engage others, inspire others, support others, develop others, and enrich others carries your legacy long after you've left.

There's one other thing. To become your best self, you must have a passion for learning. You have to be open to new experiences and open to honestly examining how you perform. You have to be willing to quickly learn from your failures, as well as your successes, and find ways to try out new behaviors without hesitation. You won't always do things perfectly, but you will get the chance to grow.

You'll get a chance to do all of that when you put *Take Charge of Your Talent* into practice. Enjoy the adventure in learning … and success.

JIM KOUZES is the coauthor of the best-selling *The Leadership Challenge* and is the Dean's Executive Fellow of Leadership, Leavey School of Business, Santa Clara University. The *Wall Street Journal* has named Jim one of the ten best executive educators in the United States, he is the recipient of the Thought Leader Award by the Instructional Systems Association, and he is one of *HR Magazine*'s Most Influential International Thinkers.

INTRODUCTION:
THE PERFECT MOMENT IS NOW

Storybook happiness involves every form of pleasant thumb-twiddling; true happiness involves the full use of one's powers and talents.

JOHN W. GARDNER

The world belongs to the talented, and that means you. If you want to take charge of your talent, enhance your career, and discover new possibilities, this book is for you. You don't need to wait for a golden opportunity or for someone else to give you the thumbs-up; you can take the initiative yourself. It's your talent, and the perfect moment is now.

Whether you're the new kid in a cubicle, you're the boss in the executive suite, or you run your own business, you have huge potential for greater productivity and fulfillment. Even very high performers in excellent organizations — large and small, for profit and nonprofit — report that 30 to 40 percent of their talent is untapped.[1] And that's only the talent they know about. It doesn't capture what they haven't discovered yet.

It doesn't matter if you are the senior manager of a big team, a teacher, a techie mastermind, or a freelancing artist. It doesn't matter if you are salaried in six figures or are just starting out. The picture is the same: *You could enjoy using more of your talent, if you could just figure out how.*

Your talent is not simply your strength or your skill set. It is your self-expression — the joyful demonstration of your unique abilities that benefit both you and the world.

1

Over the course of your life, the story about your talent can take many twists and turns. At one point, you may feel on top of the world. At other times, you may feel stuck on the sidelines. Which of the following describes where you are now?

Stymied by a hurdle, like lack of education, experience, or credentials

Lacking time and opportunities to grow

Concerned about the personal costs related to making a change

Eager and ambitious and looking for the best path

Blocked by organizational constraints

Afraid that if you tried something different, you might fail

Pigeonholed in a role you want to change

Settled, a little complacent, wondering if there is something more

Feeling fulfilled and ready to grow further

You may be itching to move forward. However, even if that's not the case and you feel at ease with the status quo, you may be missing out.

Interestingly, as authors we experienced each of the above states in the process of bringing this book to life. We felt the excitement of sharing new insights and tools. We experienced the obstacles and constraints to relaying them. We needed to navigate the fear of failure and tradeoffs with family and other interests to bring the book to completion. Fortunately, we took our own advice and employed the practices we offer in this book.

We developed the keys in this book to make talent development easy, accessible, and enjoyable for everyone. The keys are the essentials that we have distilled from decades of personal experience working in organizations as assistants, managers, and CEOs, and as professional coaches stimulating cultures of talent development. They also incorporate insights from the latest neuroscience and psychological research on how to elevate performance and satisfaction.

As powerful and effective as professional coaching can be, we became concerned that it is only accessible and affordable to less than 1 percent of the workforce. We wanted resources available for everyone. Thus, we created, tested, and optimized a simple set of keys for you to use. As our clients began to apply these keys and see the benefits, they wanted to share them with others. Some even asked, "How do we get a copy of your book?" before there actually was a book. So, here it is.

Throughout this book, you'll read the experiences and perspectives of a wide range of people, representing many different roles and workplaces. They draw from real-life situations. We've changed the names and circumstances both to protect the individuals' privacy and confidentiality and to help illustrate important points. The challenges will probably sound familiar to you. Their purpose is to help you visualize the keys in action. Ultimately, your proof will be your own experience in taking charge of your talent.

WHY YOUR TALENT MATTERS

Why should you take charge of your talent? Because your talent matters. It matters to you, it matters to your organization, and it matters to the world. When your talent lies dormant, there is a hole in your daily life. You may feel a lack of contentment and try to fill the hole with all kinds of activities and possessions that never quite do the trick. Opposing forces blunt your efforts and squash your hopes.

On the other hand, when you express your talent, the world vibrates with possibility. You feel the sweet experience of satisfaction. One idea leads to the next, and the next. Time flies. Life is filled with resources that carry you forward, sometimes in surprising ways.

Is it really that big of a deal for you to find a way to use more of your talent at work? We say "*Yes!*" It's a terrible waste when talent gets brushed aside. We know that when you aren't using your talent to the fullest, everyone pays the price. Your productivity dips, your innovation peters out, and your love of life may evaporate. You may still be doing your job, but the joy you may have had has dissipated. The frustration, boredom, or stress from work can cause toxic damage to your personal life as well. You may get in a rut and become blind to new opportunities. If you can't see the road signs, you don't take the right turns. You lose something of yourself and what you could be. Thus, the obvious makes sense: when you engage more of your talent, you become happier. And how important is that?

PUT TALENT DEVELOPMENT IN THE HANDS OF THE TALENTED

If you've gone out on your own or have recently lost your job, it may be clear to you that it's your responsibility to take charge of your talent. You need to take care of yourself, because there's nobody else who will. This book will support you in doing just that.

What if, however, you are in an organization that does give attention to talent development? Maybe *it* will take care of you. After all, enlightened organizations often have training classes and leadership development programs and give special attention to people identified as "high potentials." That's all fine and dandy, *if* you are one of the chosen ... in which case, we encourage you to take advantage of the resources that serve your aspirations. But what if you aren't one of the chosen, or you want to do more on your own initiative? We will help you to explore your talent potential more fully at work.

Even if you are one of the chosen and feel fully engaged in your work, there are strong reasons for you to take charge of your talent and for your organization to encourage you to do so. As good as top-down talent development programs in organizations may be, they have limitations for both employees and their organizations. Many start with organizational needs and train people to fill those requirements. Such programs, however, don't tap a person's core enthusiasm and accompanying talent.

How much talent gets bypassed with a mechanistic approach where each person fits into a slot and organizational objectives drive talent development? That's probably a big chunk of the 30 to 40 percent of untapped talent that employees reported in the surveys we noted earlier.

The mechanistic approach would make complete sense except that people aren't machines and don't want to be "driven" like cattle. As Daniel Pink concludes in *Drive: The Surprising Truth about What Motivates Us*, transactional systems may successfully get people to complete routine tasks, but they aren't likely to inspire the groundbreaking innovations and genuine engagement that both individuals and organizations need to thrive.[2]

When companies ask, "How do we get employees to contribute more than what's required for their pay?" they lose the race right out of the gate. This is the *transactional* view. When employees sense they are working in a tit-for-tat environment, they may respond by thinking, "OK, I've got my skills. You're my employer. How are we going to barter? What's the deal?"

The transactional mode triggers fearful behavior. Everything is a negotiation that no worker wants to lose. Yes, you want to be valued and respected. And no, you don't want to be used and taken advantage of. "What are you going to give me for my extra effort? Is it fair? Who's going to come out ahead? Who's in charge? Do I like him or her?" Even positive answers to the transactional questions lead to a dead end. What if the deal is fair? Lack of fairness can kill motivation, but fairness alone doesn't inspire it.

As a senior executive commented after his management team analyzed how best to boost results, "We concluded that we could pay people twice as much and get a short-term bump in performance, but it wouldn't make a lasting difference. Long-term change has to come from the employees' own motivation."

WHY WHAT'S GOOD FOR YOU IS GOOD FOR YOUR ORGANIZATION

Take Charge of Your Talent provides an alternative to the top-down transactional model of talent development with a new *generative* paradigm of "Everyone can play and everyone can win." This approach makes access to talent development available to all and generates an environment where people want to contribute. If your organization chooses to encourage all employees to take charge of their talent, you'll benefit from having coworkers who will be learning and growing with you.

Talent development needs to ride the wave of interest people have to take charge of what's important to them. As new opportunities arise for people to do things for themselves—for example, online brokerage or smartphone apps—generations, young and old, rush to use them. Putting talent development into the hands of the talented is similarly a movement whose time has come.

This book enables you to put the yearning to take charge into action. It offers a generative view that shifts the dynamic from "top down" to "bubble up." In the generative approach, employees are more inclined to support one another instead of competing against each other, which creates an environment that welcomes and explores fresh ideas.

Margaret Wheatley noted in *Leadership and the New Science*, "As we let go of the machine model of organizations and workers as replaceable cogs in the machinery of production, we begin to see ourselves in much richer dimensions, to appreciate our wholeness, and, hopefully, to design organizations that honor and make use of the great gift of who we humans are."[3] People can be more focused and productive in such an atmosphere because they know that they are appreciated as individuals and that the expression of their talent matters.

Maybe you're wondering, "What's in it for the boss?" Or maybe you are the boss. A brief look at employee survey data highlights the urgent need to boost employee engagement and use of talent. A Gallup employee engagement survey from 2011 reported that 71 percent of American workers were either "not engaged" in their work (emotionally detached and unlikely to be self-motivated) or "actively disengaged" (viewed their workplaces negatively and were liable to spread that negativity to others).[4] The estimated cost of actively disengaged employees in the United States alone is $400 billion to $500 billion per year.[5] Interestingly, engagement statistics have varied only a few percentage points over the last decade during both boom and bust economies.[6] And similar engagement patterns elsewhere in the world underscore the global challenge.[7,8] In short, these data demonstrate a chronic and costly problem that has remained basically unsolved.

Take Charge of Your Talent goes right to the heart of the problem with a fresh solution: tapping employee self-motivation to create authentic engagement and enduring value. The keys work at both an individual and an organizational level. They apply up, down, and across an organization and scale easily so that you can grow together efficiently and effectively. You'll learn how each employee can translate his or her talent into tangible career assets. You'll see concrete examples of how to enjoy "everyone wins" results.

Now, some managers may worry, "Will encouraging my employees to explore their own hopes for their careers prompt more people to leave and the organization to suffer?" The short answer is no. Why? Employment is a relationship. As with personal relationships, if people feel that they can't explore and grow in the relationship, they withdraw energy and commitment or pursue their interests outside the relationship. Thus, it behooves employers to encourage their employees to explore their hopes. Yes, a few people may leave, but decades of experience have shown us that the vast majority of people stay. Thoughtful conversations and engaging exercises often enable people to discover that their unexamined assumptions about limitations in the workplace were incorrect or to identify new opportunities to grow within it. The organization gains a more committed and engaged workforce.

Whether you are reading this book on your own or in an organization, you already know this fundamental truth from your life experience: *We each develop and grow most vigorously when we feel powered up.* If your engine is sputtering out or could use a boost, don't despair. It's there for you to restart—and we'll show you how.

START TURNING THE KEYS

Think of the keys in this book as your personal ignition system. Once you use the keys and get started, you can go to amazing places. What are the keys to thriving in your career, organization, and life?

Key #1: Power Up Your Talent Story. You'll gain fresh perspectives and discover resources that will support you as you become the hero of your talent story. The leaping-off place is a structured conversation that takes about an hour; it gets you in touch with powerful sources of insight and creativity that will lead you to action.

Key #2: Accelerate through Obstacles. You'll learn how to engage your talent and master frustration, discouragement, and limitations so that you can build momentum and turn your aspirations into reality. You'll gain insights into how to keep your hopes humming, fully use your resources, and take healthy stretches.

Key #3: Multiply the Payoffs for Yourself and Others. You'll convert what you know into valuable career assets that will let your talents shine and serve others. This process not only advances your personal interests but also creates a take-charge talent culture that works for everyone.

As you immerse yourself in the book, you'll find many chances to take charge of your talent. All you need to start is willingness and an open mind. For each chapter, we provide many real-life scenarios, answer critical questions, present a concise "Talent Takeaway" for you to remember, and provide clear direction with "Take Charge" actions so that you can immediately put what you read into practice. As you proceed, we want you to enjoy the process—and, dare we say, even have fun. Why? Because sustained learning and growth happen more readily when people have fun.

Unfortunately, many people don't associate developing their talents with having fun. Judgment and fear flood into our thinking: "Am I talented? Who's more talented? Will I succeed?" All of these typical reactions get in the way. Thus, it's not surprising that many people give more time, money, and attention to maintaining their cars than they do to the real engine of their success—their talent. In terms of fun, we figure that the idea of talent development probably ranks, for many people, somewhere in the neighborhood of getting your teeth cleaned. It may be important, but it's definitely not fun. So, how could this process possibly be enjoyable?

The difference is that you are in charge, and you will always remain in charge as you use the three keys. You decide how you will pursue your hopes. No one is going to drive you anywhere that you don't want to go. You will have a unique opportunity to articulate your hopes, look at your resources, and make a plan of action. While you are in charge, you won't be left adrift. You will have a catalyst and other resources to support you along the way.

Finally, you'll be able to explore on your own terms. You will be the hero of your own story. If you don't like your talent story now, change it—make it fulfilling and fun. You'll be able to share with others what you see and learn on the journey. Unlike old photos in a travelogue that fade over time, the career assets you develop will be tangible and will last. As an up-and-coming engineer commented, "This is a hoot! I mean, it's a good time."

You can start right now, right where you are, to reap benefits for your career, organization, and life.

Let's get rolling!

YOUR TAKE CHARGE CHECKLIST

Why do you want to take charge of your talent? Your reasons will be as individual as you are, and they are all valid. We've provided the checklist below for you to assess how this book can deliver what you truly want and need. Before you read about the keys to accomplishing all that, we invite you to consider which reasons resonate most for you. Which of the items on the checklist would benefit you, your organization, your family, and the rest of your life?

I want to …

- Make better use of my talent
- Gain more satisfaction from my talent
- Move forward in my career with gusto
- Know how to turn obstacles into stepping-stones
- Identify and tap the resources I need to thrive
- Develop the inner qualities I need to experience deep fulfillment
- Enjoy a better balance at work where I'm neither bored nor overloaded
- Build tangible talent assets that enhance my career and opportunities
- Make a bigger contribution to others and receive recognition for it
- Take pride in my work environment where everyone has opportunities to grow

Which of the above are true for you? Whichever reasons speak to you most, *Take Charge of Your Talent* will give you both the inspiration and the tools to create the professional life that you may have only dreamed of until now.

Key #1

POWER UP YOUR TALENT STORY

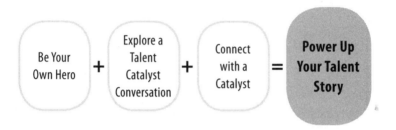

How do you start to take charge of your talent? Key #1 engages you to power up your talent story. You begin by shifting from victim of your circumstances to hero of your story. The carefully structured Talent Catalyst Conversation provides a proven way to gain a fresh perspective and stimulate new ideas. You'll learn how an appropriate person from your collection of coworkers, friends, family members, and acquaintances can be your Talent Catalyst.

Chapter 1

BE YOUR OWN HERO

Strive to live the ordinary life in an extraordinary way.
RALPH BLUM

Your talent lives inside a story. Everyone has a story about his or her talent—what it is, how he or she has used it, and what's gotten in the way. Your story works either for you or against you. It's a story of limitation or a story of possibility: the tale of a victim or the tale of a hero. The victim story is one of fear, moving away from new possibilities, being stuck, and staying put. The hero story is one of hope, obstacles overcome, and action. It is a story of new chapters, fresh energy, getting unstuck, and taking charge. At some time or another throughout our lives, we have all probably played both roles, knowingly or not.

Since no one wants to be the victim of his or her story, it's good news that the hero story can belong to all of us, not just a golden few. Most of us think of heroes as those extraordinary people who have almost magical abilities. Capes and super powers may even come to mind. For this book's purposes, when we talk about being the hero of your talent story, we refer to everyday heroes—people who take action in the face of their fears and move toward their hopes to enjoy practical results.

RECLAIM THE POWER IN YOUR STORY

It may seem strange to think of your talent as a story. You may be saying to yourself, "My situation isn't just a story. It's the hard and cold reality that I live." That's true. The facts are what they are. But pause for a moment to consider the idea that your *interpretation* of those facts is a story. Changing your interpretation can make all the difference.

Between coaching and delivering talent development workshops, we have met thousands of people and have heard their stories. Let's look at the situations of some typical people who began with some frustration about their circumstances or hunger for change and transformed their stories using the keys in this book:

> Fran: "I want to be a supervisor and know I'm ready, but the supervisory job opportunities require prior managerial experience. I'm stuck."
>
> Sheila: "I want to work on bigger projects that will bring more value to our business, but as a financial services manager, my plate is so full and I've pushed my team so far that I don't see any way. I can't spend more time at work; my family would really suffer, and so would I."
>
> Miguel: "I have much more that I could contribute to our IT firm, but rising higher in the leadership would compromise time with my family and require me to be too political. I'll keep my head down and continue plugging away at my current role. I guess it's better to be a little bored."
>
> Nadia: "I've been given a great opportunity to restructure our health care organization and want to take advantage of it, but I'm struggling to lead the way I want to."
>
> Ben: "I really wanted this job and started with lots of energy and ideas, but now I'm totally at the mercy of the bureaucracy. I want to teach and show the kids that learning is great, but how can I do that with all the regulations and tests?"

Kim: "I'm not sure I have the talent to pull off this presentation. What am I doing on the same stage with these expert scientists and this CEO? I will probably fail and look stupid."

Tony: "My problem is that everyone just sees me as a police chief, when I feel ready for broader opportunities in local government. I can't break out to grow."

Jesse: "Many people envy my position, but the fact is that I'm a little bored. Unless my boss dies or retires, this is it."

Do you see something of your situation in any of these stories, or maybe in several? What does your story read like at this time?

Each of these stories is true in the sense that the circumstances are real. In fact, the stories provide some comfort for the people who hold them. They describe circumstances—situations, other people, or even requirements—that keep these persons from greater fulfillment of their talent. It gets them off the hook for taking responsibility. As a result, they have a ready response to coworkers, friends, and family members who ask, "What's happening with your job?" The answer is simple: "I'm stuck." In fact, they may even find sympathy from others. They might hear comments like "Yeah, the requirements are unfair. How could anyone expect you to move forward?" "Boy, the economic downturn is really hitting your business. You're lucky to just hold on to what you have." "You do have an overwhelming workload. I don't know how you do it."

Thus, there are many reasons for people to hold on to their stories and to keep their circumstances fixed, even immutable, in their minds. But is that how these stories must continue or, worse, end? Are the characters—are you—stuck in a rut without hope for change?

In each of these talent stories, people have given their power to someone or something else. Indeed, they have become merely players in the stories about other people, their organizations, or economic circumstances.

To create new and more fulfilling chapters in your talent story, you need to take back the lead, the power, of your story. You need to be your own hero. In fact, you are the only person who can be the hero of your talent story. If you're not the hero of your own story, you simply become a player in one you didn't choose.

Now, many of us don't think of ourselves as heroes. The role sounds too big, too risky, or just not us. That might be true in terms of being a hero on the battlefield, in politics, or while attempting some world-saving feat. However, you *can* be the hero of your talent story. We'll show you how and give you examples of everyday people who have done just that.

HOW DO HEROES OF TALENT STORIES ACT?

We all love heroes, especially those who rise from being seemingly everyday people. While they may be ordinary folks, something sets them apart. Heroes act differently because they learn to think differently. Heroes are ordinary people who are willing to go beyond their perceived limitations. They see the potential for growth and change in themselves and their circumstances.

> **Heroes have hopes.** Heroes have hopes and are willing to do ethically what it takes to realize them. Every hero has fears too. Heroes confront their fears and act on their hopes. If they are on course and confront obstacles, they use their talents to find a way to deal with them. However, in the end, they keep moving forward.

> **Heroes recognize opportunities.** Heroes look for opportunities. Where others see dead ends, heroes see possibilities. When heroes see inroads, they take them. If they don't see a way in, they enlist others to help create new solutions.

> **Heroes act.** Even when others are afraid to get involved and

prefer to play it safe and watch from a distance, heroes find ways to make steady progress toward their objectives.

It's important to note that heroes are not rabid risk takers. While they are willing to try new approaches, they (or the people who support them) usually have a keen sense of risk and opportunity. Indeed, some of the biggest risk takers, Silicon Valley venture capitalists, focus on how to wring risk out of new ventures to help them succeed. Therefore, we're not suggesting that you bet the farm to develop and apply your talent. It's your story. You'll get to write it how you wish. We will help you to explore the healthy stretches that can lead to heroic results for you.

HOW TAKING A HERO'S ROLE CHANGES EVERYTHING

Let's look at how the people you met before might reframe their talent stories in simple, practical ways to become their own heroes.

What if Fran could communicate her hopes to a boss or friend and find a way to begin acting like the supervisor she wants to be, right from where she is?

What if there were hidden opportunities for Sheila to work with her team and delegate responsibilities so she could branch out into using her talent to create more value for herself and the organization?

What if Miguel could rise in the organization without compromising his personal and family values?

What if Nadia were to discover that she is struggling in her new leadership position only because she is trying to be someone she's not?

What if Ben could find a way to stay passionate about his work and remain productive in spite of the bureaucracy?

What if Kim could use her unique abilities and resources instead of comparing herself with others?

What if Tony could document his broader skills and rebrand himself as a leader guiding innovation in tough budget times?

What if Jesse could shift from thinking his career is set to finding new ways to grow?

Do these what-ifs sound plausible to you? Each of them actually happened. Each of them began with an openness to see the current story as something that the person was willing to look at in a new way. Each of them occurred because the person was willing to explore how he or she might become the hero of his or her own talent story.

BE THE HERO OF YOUR TALENT STORY

Maybe you don't want to wait for someone else to come along and make everything right for you. Maybe you don't want to wait for a golden opportunity or to inherit money from an as-yet-unknown source or to be picked by others to move forward or to wait for your boss to retire or die so that you can advance.

Everything we offer in this book is for people who are ready to be the heroes of their talent stories. The hero story can belong to all of us, not just a chosen few. It doesn't matter what your story is or what your circumstances are. If you are seriously stuck and hate your job, or if you are hoping to make more of the satisfying career you already have, the keys are one and the same.

No matter who you are or what your situation is, it all comes down to one point: you always have a choice. You get to decide *how* you are going to play out your talent story and your role in it. Unless you default and give the power to someone else, it's yours to decide.

When we make choices that are in accord with our hopes and desires, we generally feel good and get a surge of energy and commitment that comes from being in alignment and taking charge. This is not to say that we won't have to deal with tough situations along the road. We all do. But when we hold true to our hopes, we can take the bumps. We'll talk more in depth about that later.

Is your "current" story ironclad? Can any story be changed for the good? Can you really turn it around and create a story that works for you? Evidence shows that anyone can change his or her story permanently. But you'll have to be willing to open up to possibilities.

As the hero of your own story, you are the singular beginning point.

We realize that it may seem daunting to see your talent as a story you can change and to position yourself as the hero within it. Perhaps you are thinking, "You don't understand how limiting my situation is. I truly am stuck, and the tradeoffs feel too big." Or "I'd like to explore these ideas, but this is a whole new way of looking at myself and my career. How do I make this concrete for myself?" Good questions.

The next chapters will make this process clear for you. You'll learn about a carefully designed conversation that in the span of about an hour will enable you to begin dictating the talent story you want to pursue—one with you in the lead. We'll guide you to connect with an appropriate friend, coworker, family member, or acquaintance who will be your catalyst for new insights, opportunities, and actions and will help you to identify resources to realize them. These tools started the people in this chapter on their new paths.

TALENT TAKEAWAY

Your talent is a story you can transform. When you position yourself as the hero of your story and follow a clear set of actions to act out that role, your career and life can change and move forward quickly.

TAKE CHARGE

You may feel that you want to change your talent story, but since change can be scary, you might find yourself dragging your feet. If so, try this:

Make two lists on separate pieces of paper, one titled "Benefits I See for Keeping My Current Story," the other titled "Benefits I Foresee in Becoming the Hero of My Story." When you are done, read them aloud several times. Then choose which story you want to live by, and post the list in a prominent place. Throw the other list away. The choice is yours.

Chapter 2

EXPLORE A TALENT CATALYST CONVERSATION

*The basic difference between human beings and other species is
that we live in a world that is created by the stories we tell.*

GEORGE GERBNER

We all need fresh perspective at times—but it's hard to see
life in a new light if we are groping around in the dark for the
switch. The Talent Catalyst Conversation is the switch to help
you to identify new possibilities and shine light on your situation. Amazing things can happen when you decide to engage
your talent, and the first step is to recognize that you are the
author of a story you can change—for good.

Let's take a look at Ben's story. Ben felt as if his life were set
in stone. "I dreamed of being a teacher and helping others get
ahead like my teachers helped me years ago. But I had no idea
that I'd be struggling under the administrative details, standardized test pressures, and internal politics that consume so much
of my energy and sap my passion for this job. My teaching job
pays OK, and if I can stick it out to retirement, I'll have a decent
pension. I guess I'll just keep my head down and gut it out, but
that feels like giving up on myself and my dreams."

Ben's not alone. We hear stories from people in corporations,
government agencies, hospitals, and small businesses who face
similar challenges. They are the walking wounded—capable
and motivated people who feel held back from pursuing their
hopes and aspirations. They worry that their vigor and spirit is
slowly dying in them, but it's not clear what they can do to halt

the process. Many people try to console them: "Hey, welcome to the real world." Loved ones may feel anxious for them and even for themselves: "Look, it keeps a roof over our heads and food on the table. In this economy, you don't want to rock the boat." Yet others rail against the machine: "You ought to organize and fight back. Show them that they can't boss you around." While any one of these responses is reasonable and human, they don't change the everyday reality for people like Ben or give him something he can do right now to make a positive change.

The fifty minutes that Ben spent in his Talent Catalyst Conversation opened new energy, new ideas, and actionable opportunities for him. Instead of cramming down the hopes and dreams that drew him to his work, the Conversation started with an exploration of his hopes and why they are important to him. Ben commented, "I can't remember anyone else asking me about my hopes, at least not in a work setting. All that people typically talk about around here are the performance expectations they have for us and our students. I really felt myself becoming alive again."

He remembered the eagerness and energy he previously had for the profession. He also remembered his successes during college in gracefully navigating the bureaucracy of local government and village politics to get a community center built in a struggling African city. Most important, the questions invited him to identify ways to translate his talent for engaging disadvantaged students in programs he could offer to other teachers and school systems hungering for fresh material—and to earn some extra money for himself as well. "I realized that I have insights and experiences I can package into something tangible that others will value. I realized I can do more of what makes me passionate about this profession."

Did Ben's efforts change public school policies? No, but as his talents flowed, he gained more energy and even joined a task force on school reform. He got the programs for disadvantaged students up and running—and administrators around the county were taking notice. "I'm feeling charged up again. I feel like I'm making a difference and have my old 'get up and go' again."

Will your Conversation have the transformative effects that Ben and many others have enjoyed? We're confident that it will, but you'll soon find out for yourself. We simply want you to see enough potential that you are willing to connect with a Talent Catalyst and experience the Conversation for yourself.

Some people wonder, "I'm not sure exactly what I'd talk about in the Conversation. Maybe I'd better wait until I have my thoughts together before I have one of these Talent Catalyst Conversations."

Don't wait. The Talent Catalyst Conversation helps you to *figure out what's important to you* and where you want to go. If you already had everything figured out in your head and your talent optimized, you wouldn't need a Talent Catalyst Conversation. And there are no right or wrong answers to the questions about your hopes, opportunities, and actions. They are simply your answers. Thus, you can't fail.

"But what if the Conversation goes in some unexpected directions that I don't feel comfortable talking about? Will I have opened a Pandora's Box?" No. First, *you* pick the topic for the Talent Catalyst Conversation. It can be about ways to make your work more productive or fulfilling, how you might move forward, the legacy you'd like to leave in your profession, or any of a host of other topics. You choose what you'd like to address. Second, you pick *who* will be your Talent Catalyst. In the next chapter, we explain that important role in more detail and provide guidelines to help you choose an appropriate person. Finally, you choose *what you say* and the ideas and actions you explore. And we emphasize "explore." It's understood that you are exploring opportunities and directions. You can decide after the Conversation how you want to apply the results of it.

The Talent Catalyst Conversation Guide in this chapter gives you and the person who will be asking you the carefully designed questions (your Talent Catalyst) the information needed to enjoy a productive Conversation. The Conversation consists of three rounds, which frame the Conversation around the elements necessary to construct your hero's story: hopes, opportunities, and actions. The steps and questions target what will bring forth your best thinking in a constructive way. Thus, you'll want to follow them closely. Otherwise, it's easy to fall off into fearful thinking or distractions that will undermine your success. (Note: Chapters 4, 5, and 6, which address ongoing practices to implement the results of your Talent Catalyst Conversation, discuss the neuroscience, psychological, and experiential underpinnings for the framework.)

Read the Talent Catalyst Conversation Guide to become acquainted with how the Conversation works. Don't develop fixed answers in advance of your actual conversation, however. Such overpreparation will likely further commit you to your current thinking and make your mental ruts even deeper. As the Talent Catalyst reflects your responses and helps you to follow your hopes, new ideas and options will arise on the spot.

The Talent Catalyst Conversation Guide follows. It's set up so that you can pick it up and use it with a Talent Catalyst. The Conversation has no hidden agendas. We suggest that both the Talent Catalyst and participant read the Guide before having a Conversation. For further insights, see "Frequently Asked Questions about the Talent Catalyst Conversation" in the "Resources" section at the back of the book. For an illustration of a Conversation, see the "Sample Talent Catalyst Conversation and Summary," which also resides in the "Resources" section.

TALENT CATALYST CONVERSATION GUIDE

The Talent Catalyst Conversation involves a process of thoughtful dialogue between two partners in which one person plays the role of the participant and the other serves as the Talent Catalyst. The carefully structured information and the questions that the

Talent Catalyst asks help the participant to clarify hopes, opportunities, and actions that he or she may choose to pursue. After completing the Conversation, you can reverse the roles, either in the same sitting, at a future time, or with different partners. In this way, each person has the opportunity to unlock his or her own talents as a participant and to give to someone else as a Talent Catalyst. When people experience both roles, they deepen their skills, strengthen collegiality, and build a sustainable, shared culture of talent development.

Being a Talent Catalyst

The fact that anyone can be a Talent Catalyst opens the field for who can serve in this important role. It can be a novice—a supervisor, coworker, colleague, friend, or family member—or a trained Talent Catalyst. The critical issue is not who the Talent Catalyst is but how he or she follows the Guide and fulfills the role. Here's a summary of the behaviors that are critical for a Talent Catalyst to serve successfully.

Keep a Participant Focus

Remember that the role of the Talent Catalyst is to precipitate action and accelerate results by helping the participant to sort through his or her thoughts and target ways to realize what the participant wants. It is not to make the Conversation be about the Catalyst or what the Catalyst wants. This gives the Talent Catalyst enormous freedom to reflect what's heard and support the participant. It also frees the participant from feeling that he or she must impress or prove something to the Talent Catalyst. So, the Talent Catalyst needs to keep the Conversation focused on the participant.

The Talent Catalyst offers ideas or suggestions only after the participant has responded to the questions and then only after asking the participant if he or she would like additional ideas or suggestions. This ensures that the participant stays in charge and the Talent Catalyst isn't emotionally drained by feeling responsible for the participant's choices.

Let the participant go where his or her thoughts and motivation lead the Conversation. If, as Talent Catalyst, you have a preset agenda or outcome for the Conversation (for example, an outcome you want the participant to produce or an action you want the participant to take), it will undermine the Conversation's effectiveness and the participant's ownership of the results and self-motivation to follow through and get results.

Be clear about how you will handle confidentiality of the Conversation so that the participant can be as candid as possible.

Employ Generous Listening

Generous listening demonstrates curiosity, a suspension of judgment and evaluation, and a desire to understand both the meaning and the motivation of the participant. After the participant responds to a question, reflect what you've heard. Before you go any further, be sure to check in and see if you are hearing what the participant intended. You will be serving the process by reflecting what you hear so that the participant knows that he or she has been heard. This also helps the participant to clarify thoughts and communication.

Follow the Structured Questions

The carefully designed and proven questions help the participant to develop his or her own story with a focus on hopes, opportunities, and actions. Unless you stick with the structure, it's easy for the Talent Catalyst to unwittingly editorialize or otherwise distract the participant's focus. Think of the Talent Catalyst as a reporter trying to capture the facts from the participant without distortion.

After review of these criteria for a Talent Catalyst, confirm whether the person is an appropriate match for the particular participant. If "yes," proceed to the following.

Getting Started

A Talent Catalyst can be someone the participant knows well or has just met. Let's assume you are meeting for the first time or are not well acquainted.

Become Acquainted

If you don't know one another, take a few moments to become acquainted. A brief thumbnail sketch from each person will do fine. The Talent Catalyst doesn't need to know many details about the participant. Important information will arise as needed in the Conversation. Similarly, the Talent Catalyst and participant don't need to impress one another with what they know or have accomplished. That's not the purpose of the Conversation.

Identify the Focus for the Conversation

In which area would the participant like to boost his or her use of talent and level of satisfaction? Often, it's about use of talent in a job or career. Sometimes it's about a talent for personal use; it could even be about talent in handling relationships. Choose a particular area so that you have a focus for the immediate Conversation. You can have Conversations on the other topics at another time.

Doing the Conversation: Step-by-Step

The Talent Catalyst Conversation consists of ten steps that are organized into three rounds that track the critical components of hopes, opportunities, and actions. You can proceed straight through all the ten steps in the Conversation or use the rounds as convenient break points, as needed. When you follow the script, the complete Talent Catalyst Conversation typically takes between forty-five minutes and an hour. We encourage you to keep the Conversation moving. Participants and Talent Catalysts have found that a pace of about five minutes or so per step works well. If the participant gets stuck on a particular step, there is no need to dwell on it. Feel free to move on, as it is the sum of the steps that creates the impact, more than any one step in particular. Valuable insights and breakthroughs can occur at any point. Remember that the "Frequently Asked Questions about the Talent Catalyst Conversation" and "Sample Talent Catalyst Conversation and Summary" (see the "Resources" section) are available, as needed, to boost your understanding and confidence in having a Conversation.

Decide who (participant or Talent Catalyst) will read aloud the introduction for each step as you proceed. Then the Talent Catalyst asks the first question, reflects what the participant says, and proceeds to the follow-up question(s) for the step. It's extremely useful to have the Talent Catalyst take some notes about the participant's responses to each question. This gives the participant some valuable notes to review afterward without having to edit his or her thoughts along the way.

Ready?

Round I: Enliven Your Hopes

This round helps the participant to focus on what's important, consider concerns, and build confidence in the prospects for success. In short, it initiates the participant's constructive thinking to tap the creativity and motivation to move forward.

Step 1: Connect with Your Hopes

You need energy to make positive changes in your life. When you connect with your deepest hopes (that is, your interests and aspirations about the topic you've chosen), the energy you produce will help you to see possibilities and opportunities around you with more clarity. You will be more likely to make sound, creative choices that lead to better use of your talents; greater personal satisfaction; and more powerful contributions to your family, community, team, and organization.

What are your hopes about the topic you've chosen for this Conversation?

Why are your hopes important to you?

Cues for the Catalyst: For each step, ask the first question, reflect what you hear, confirm that you've heard what the participant intended, and then proceed in the same way with the follow-up question. As you explore these initial questions, you are helping the participant to tap into personal wisdom and creative talent. Listen for and reflect back both what the participant is saying and anything you notice about changes in tone of voice, energy, and emotions. People don't often think about their hopes. The participant may need a few moments to think about the question. Confirm what you hear about the participant's deepest aspirations for the topic.

Step 2: Consider Your Concerns

When we focus on our deepest hopes, our brain often attempts to protect us from harm by generating stories of concern. Ignoring them could be dangerous; yet assuming they can't be overcome will also limit what is possible. For now, we suggest that you simply acknowledge their presence.

What's standing between you and realizing your hopes?

Which of your concerns seems most important to address now so that you can make progress toward your hopes?

Cues for the Catalyst: Reflect the concerns you hear without agreeing with them, disputing them, or trying to fix them. For example, "I hear that [concern] feels like the most immediate one you'd like to address. Is that correct?"

Step 3: Tap Your Success Stories

We can look to the past to see how we have successfully dealt with similar concerns. Retrieving memories of past successes can provide clues to overcoming current issues, situations, or concerns.

> How have you successfully dealt with concerns like these before?
>
> What did you learn from the situation that might help you now?

Cues for the Catalyst: If the participant has a success story, reflect and acknowledge his or her ability to deal with the kinds of concerns that have surfaced in this Conversation. If a personal success story does not come to the participant's mind, reflect that and ask if there is a story the participant can imagine or has seen or heard about how others have successfully dealt with the situation.

Round II: Expand Your Opportunities

While your success stories may provide some approaches that you can build upon, significant progress requires new growth and learning. This round focuses on growth and learning, as well as the resources and expanded hopes that will help you to develop your talent. Note that chapter 5 explores these issues more deeply. For now, you are developing an outline that will focus further thinking and action.

Step 4: Identify Opportunities to Learn, Grow, and Develop

As you work toward realizing your hopes, you will have many opportunities to learn, grow, and develop. This growth may be in knowledge, skills, or inner qualities like curiosity, assertiveness, or compassion. This process is likely to be energizing and pleasurable, as it opens up fresh possibilities to express your talent more fully.

> How will you need to grow, and what will you need to learn to address your concerns and realize your hopes?

> What inner qualities may you need to develop to support you?

Cues for the Catalyst: Ask the participant to zero in on areas of growth (for example, targeted knowledge, specific skills, or particular attributes) that are essential to his or her desired success. Feel free to reflect the emotion you hear, whether it be enthusiasm or hesitance, to help identify the focus.

Step 5: Use Your Resources

Resources feed our hopes. Everything we accomplish, we accomplish by using our resources: the people, places, and things that surround us and the capabilities within us. Often, concerns arise because we worry that we lack the resources to realize our hopes: "I hope to do X, but I don't have enough of Y [time, money, connections, ideas, education, skill, space, etc.]." When we recognize the abundance of our resources, our brain responds with a sense of possibility. We are emotionally, energetically, and creatively in a great place to move into our future.

> What resources do you have that can help you to realize your hopes?

> How can you use these resources?

Cues for the Catalyst: This will likely be an ongoing process for the participant. The participant doesn't have to come up with a complete list on the spot, but it will be helpful if he or she identifies enough resources to feel that realizing the targeted hopes is a real possibility. If you have relevant possibilities to offer, ask if the participant would like you to offer your ideas as well.

Step 6: Revisit Your Hopes

Time to check back in with your hopes. Remember, we suggested that when you connect with your deepest hopes, the energy you produce will help you to see possibilities and opportunities around you with more clarity. You may wish to revise your hopes, either by articulating them in a different way or by prioritizing differently.

> At this point in the Conversation, do you have some greater clarity about your hopes?

> How would you express your hopes now?

Cues for the Catalyst: Your job as a catalyst is to help ignite a spark. Continue to listen for and reflect what you sense the participant is feeling. This will help inspire constructive thinking and make it much more likely that these hopes will inspire action. If you hear new hopes, explore why those are important to the participant.

Round III: Energize Yourself through Actions

It's time for action! However, before you launch off with the first idea that comes to mind, this round invites you to consider a healthy stretch you might like to make: an objective you can reach for that is challenging without causing unproductive stress or pain. Then it proceeds to who can support you and the actions you'd like to take to get started.

Step 7: Make a Healthy Stretch

One path to engage your talents is to honestly and joyfully make a stretch. This approach loses its power if the participant undertakes a stretch out of obligation or duty. You don't need to know in advance how you would accomplish the stretch. After this Conversation, you can follow the guidance in chapter 6 to pursue your desired stretch successfully.

What might a healthy stretch look like in your situation?

Is there something that you could start doing now to enjoy greater fulfillment of your hopes?

Cues for the Catalyst: Listen for and reflect both the words and the emotions you hear. If the participant is stuck, you can ask permission to offer a stretch, but if you do not hear an enthusiastic response, just let it go. This step is an opportunity, not a requirement.

Step 8: Enlist a Talent Fulfillment Team for Results

Imagine that you have a Talent Fulfillment Team of people who can support and inspire you. The world is full of people who can bring out your best and fill in your gaps of knowledge, skill, experience, and expertise. These can be people already in your circle and others beyond it. Think as big as you'd like. Later you can use the "Enlist Your Talent Fulfillment Team" section in chapter 6 for guidance on how to reach and engage the people you seek.

Who would be ideal to have on your team?

Who could help you to play as big as you'd like?

Can you visualize these people cheering for you as you fulfill your hopes?

Cues for the Catalyst: Listen for any situation in which the participant is placing limits on who can be on the team. If you have possibilities, ask if the participant would welcome your suggestions as well.

Step 9: Target Concrete Actions

Critical to any success is taking appropriate, concrete actions. Take some small actions or make a big leap. Either way, *act*!

What forward-moving actions would you enjoy taking now toward realizing your hopes?

Cues for the Catalyst: Listen for and reflect what you hear the participant really wants to do. Notice and reflect anything that sounds like an obligation or a "should do." If you have additional options to consider, ask if the participant would like you to offer them. Do not take it personally if the participant does not accept your ideas or commit to what you think would be better to do. The participant is in charge.

Step 10: Reflect on Your Possibilities and Progress

Take a few minutes to digest the experience you've just had. As participants explore these questions with thoughtful Talent Catalysts, they often gain insights and identify opportunities and actions in the Conversation itself. For other participants, the Conversation creates ripples that may require more time to demonstrate their effects.

What have you gained from this Conversation?

What will help you to follow through on your intentions?

Cues for the Catalyst: Acknowledge any fresh ideas that the participant may have and what he or she may want to do to make them happen. Know that whatever progress the participant has or hasn't made, you've fulfilled your role as a Talent Catalyst. When participants truly own these Conversations, the benefits continue to arise over time.

Below is a summary form for the notes the Talent Catalyst takes for the participant. A complete conversation is shown in "Sample Talent Catalyst Conversation and Summary" in "Resources."

SUMMARY NOTES FOR YOUR TALENT CATALYST CONVERSATION

Summary of Round I: Enliven Your Hopes

1. Hopes

2. Concerns

3. Success Stories

Summary of Round II: Expand Your Opportunities

4. Opportunities

5. Resources

   PEOPLE

   PLACES

   THINGS/INNER QUALITIES

6. Hopes Revisited

Summary of Round III: Energize Yourself through Actions

7. Healthy Stretch

8. Talent Fulfillment Team

9. Actions

10. Reflections on Possibilities and Progress

TALENT TAKEAWAY

Enjoy a Talent Catalyst Conversation. It's a gift for you. Explore how it can help you to change your talent story for good.

TAKE CHARGE

Choose a topic about your talent that you'd like to explore through a Talent Catalyst Conversation. Where would you like to do more with your talent or enjoy it more? You don't need to specify your topic perfectly. You can even have multiple Talent Catalyst Conversations with different people to explore a number of different topics. Now that you have a feel for what the Conversation is like, go to the next chapter to learn more about connecting with someone who can serve as a Talent Catalyst for you.

Chapter 3

CONNECT WITH A CATALYST

To listen well is as powerful a means of influence as to talk well,
and is as essential to all true conversation.

CHINESE PROVERB

Fran was having a hard time changing her talent story. She needed help. She wanted to see herself from a fresh perspective, but she was unsure how. She felt frustrated and stuck. She met her friend Jules at a café, hoping to come up with options. As soon as Fran sat down and started talking, Jules took out his cell phone and sent a quick text and then fiddled with his watch. Fran ignored her friend's inattention and plunged into the details. Jules gazed out the window and said, "Uh-huh." Finally, he looked up at Fran, but his mind was somewhere else as he did the seven-mile stare. Fran braved on, "I'm stuck. Every management job I look at requires prior supervisory experience. There's just no way around it."

"Yeah," said Jules, "I never liked your boss—what a jerk. Want my advice? Quit and work in a better office where you could be a supervisor. I mean, everyone likes you."

"But I like the people I work with. My boss isn't the issue, Jules," replied Fran. "I've checked every position within our organization over the last six months, and they all have that prerequisite. I'm just stuck."

"Yeah, I hate that. I feel stuck at work, too. Maybe you should just be grateful that you have a reliable job in this crappy economy. Besides, you like to paint. You can always focus on that when you're not at work. And at least you have Jim — he's so supportive. I don't have anyone," lamented Jules.

Chances are, you have been in a conversation like this yourself. Fran can see no way to change her story. Jules is not present to hear Fran and doesn't know how to be a generous listener. He doesn't apply the focus and skills needed to help his friend get out of the loop of frustration.

Of course, it isn't just Jules's inattention that keeps Fran stuck. Did you hear how she held on to her story even when it didn't serve her — and how Jules reinforced it, as well? Psychologists call this pattern the resolution of cognitive dissonance. When people have beliefs, as evidenced by their stories, and receive information that doesn't fit with their stories, they discount it. This protects the point of view to which they have become committed. As an old saying goes, "The only person who wants to *be changed* is a wet baby."

The reality, however, is that people do change when they have the *choice to change*. Look at how quickly people can learn. Technophobes all over the world handle their smartphones like aces. People chose to change for the benefits they got from using this new technology, not because someone required them to change.

How can you get the fresh perspective you need the next time you're stuck and want to create a new chapter of your talent story? We'd like to introduce you to the Talent Catalyst. This is a person who will listen to you and reflect your own thoughts back to you so that you can clarify your hopes and begin to discover ways to take action to move toward them. The Talent Catalyst helps you to stop the repeating loop of fear or worry that is not serving you. What makes the role of Talent Catalyst different from good-intentioned well-wishers is that the person serving in a Talent Catalyst role doesn't give advice. Instead, the Talent Catalyst agrees to hear you, help you to hear yourself, and support what you hope to achieve. The Catalyst sets aside any personal agenda or stake in your choices.

Let's take a deeper look.

WHAT IS A TALENT CATALYST?

A Talent Catalyst is just what it sounds like—a spark, in the form of a person who wakes you up to new possibilities through the course of your conversation with the person. Your Talent Catalyst doesn't need hours of training. He or she just needs to be willing to follow the structured Talent Catalyst Conversation Guide provided in the previous chapter and to play the role.

We model the Talent Catalyst on the metaphor of a catalyst in chemistry. Like catalysts in chemical reactions, Talent Catalysts accelerate your thinking and activate results. Notably, like chemical catalysts, Talent Catalysts don't get used up in the process. This is important because their formal commitment ends after the prescribed Conversation, leaving them without the burden of feeling responsible for your progress. They stay energized, and you stay in charge of your talent.

What makes the engagement of a Talent Catalyst so transformative? Certainly, it's helpful to have someone reflect your thoughts back to you, enabling you to see yourself from a new viewpoint and hear your own thoughts spoken out loud. But after witnessing more than a thousand Talent Catalyst Conversations, we see that Talent Catalysts do much more than mirror what you express. Even among relative strangers, Talent Catalysts initiate a deeper human connection that stimulates action and precipitates results.

We're delving more deeply into the role of the Talent Catalyst for three reasons. When you learn more about the benefits of the role, you may feel more at ease and eager to go forward with a Talent Catalyst Conversation. Also, details about the role will help you to identify an appropriate person to serve as your Talent Catalyst. Finally, as you see the distinctive role of the Talent Catalyst and the value of the skills it builds, you may gain the motivation to serve as a Talent Catalyst for others.

ESSENTIAL ATTRIBUTES OF A TALENT CATALYST

What makes an effective Talent Catalyst? An effective Catalyst is willing to participate, asks carefully structured open-ended questions, engages in generous listening, and lets the participant be in charge. Let's take a look at these elements in more detail.

Is a Willing Partner

Have you ever tried to have a conversation with someone who was distracted like Jules? How did that feel? Probably not great. The first and most important requirement of a Talent Catalyst is that the person gives you full attention during your conversation. And since you're not just having a casual chat, he or she needs to be able to stay focused on following the script and to abide by the guidelines. Similarly, as the participant, you need to be willing to show up and be open to new ideas.

Asks Carefully Structured, Open-Ended Questions

It is essential to the Talent Catalyst Conversation that the Catalyst ask open-ended questions—questions designed to encourage a full answer beyond yes or no. In contrast, closed-ended questions limit responses or manipulate:

> Would you like to go to the swimming pool this afternoon?
>
> Can you have it on my desk by Friday?
>
> Are you ready to take on some added responsibility? [Would there be a consequence if the person said no?]
>
> You don't want to disappoint her, do you? [Can you spell g-u-i-l-t t-r-i-p?]

Open-ended questions encourage full, thoughtful answers—for example:

> How would you enjoy spending the afternoon?

What would it take to have it on my desk by Friday?

What changes would you like to see in your job description?

What's the best way to settle this so that both sides feel good about it?

We've made it easy for the Talent Catalyst to ask open-ended questions of you because this is the form of questions used in the Talent Catalyst Conversation Guide.

Not just any open-ended questions are appropriate, however. Your Talent Catalyst needs to follow the carefully structured questions presented in the Guide. "Why?" you may ask. "I thought this was a dialogue or brainstorming kind of thing." No. It's not. As you saw in the snippet of dialogue between Fran and Jules, his well-intentioned questions and comments actually locked Fran deeper into her story about being stuck. She felt that she needed to defend herself rather than think creatively. Typical conversations fall back into such dynamics. They won't work to help you change your story.

Is a Generous Listener

Most of us think we're pretty good listeners. To be effective Talent Catalysts, people need to listen in fresh ways. Here are three *ineffective* ways of listening:

Listen mindlessly. Pay little or no attention to the speaker and assume that you know what the speaker means even before he or she has finished speaking.

Listen selfishly. Pay particular attention to what's in it for you; judge and evaluate the speaker and his or her views; and wait, not always patiently, for a chance to tell your own story: "That reminds me of a time when I … ," "Oh, I know what you mean, because my cousin once … "

Listen "wisely." Listening to the situation so that you can provide your wisdom and counsel may seem like a generous thing to do, but it runs counter to the purpose of the Talent Catalyst. The Talent Catalysts are there to help participants access their inner wisdom, not to show off their own.

Curiosity, a suspension of judgment and evaluation, and a desire to understand both the meaning and the motivation of the speaker distinguish generous listening from everyday listening. Generous listeners reflect what they've heard and take time to check in and see if it's what the participant intended to communicate. The Talent Catalyst serves the process by letting the participant know that he or she is being heard and by helping the participant to clarify his or her communication if there is a disconnect. Here are three ways in which a Catalyst can reflect effectively what the participant says:

Reflect the words. Simply repeat or paraphrase the words that the participant said. This may sound awfully basic, but you will be surprised at how beautifully it gives the speaker a chance to clarify his or her own thoughts.

Reflect the feeling. Let the speaker know what emotion you hear in his or her communication. "It sounds like you may be feeling some frustration in your current role."

Reflect the speaker's hope or need. "Are you saying that you need a bigger challenge?"

Any one of these reflections will keep the Conversation on track and moving forward. Here's what it might sound like if the Talent Catalyst used all three types of reflection together:

PARTICIPANT: I've been in the same position now for three years, and it's not as enjoyable as it used to be.

TALENT CATALYST: So you've been in the same position for

three years and aren't enjoying it anymore. Are you feeling frustrated and eager to have a bigger challenge?

PARTICIPANT: Yes, that's it.

In this case, the Talent Catalyst heard exactly what the speaker was trying to communicate and helped the participant to move forward. But the Talent Catalyst needn't worry about getting it wrong. Reflecting gives the participant the chance to expand on a short or unclear answer. What might it have sounded like if the Talent Catalyst had misinterpreted the participant's message?

PARTICIPANT: I've been in the same position now for three years, and it's not as enjoyable as it used to be.

TALENT CATALYST: So you've been in the same position for three years and aren't enjoying it anymore. Are you feeling frustrated and eager to have a bigger challenge?

PARTICIPANT: No, that's not really it. When I started, there were three of us in the department. With the cutbacks, I'm the only one left. I don't really enjoy working alone.

TALENT CATALYST: Oh, I see. Cutbacks have left you on your own, and you prefer working with others.

PARTICIPANT: Yes, that's it exactly. I want to get back to working with other people.

The power of generous listening prompts us to think that much more than simply reflective listening occurs in these Conversations.[1] What distinguishes generous listening from basic reflective listening is the Talent Catalyst's commitment to hold or champion the participant's hopes.

Perhaps something of the transformative catalytic effect of generous listening arises not only from the act of listening but also from an unconscious connection between participant and Talent Catalyst. This connection may boost the participant's perception and help the participant to access otherwise hidden inner resources and otherwise inaccessible solutions to seemingly deep-end problems. Recent research into the role of mirror neurons suggests the potential for deep exchanges of insights and wisdom. As Daniel Goleman notes in *The Brain and Emotional Intelligence: New Insights*, mirror neurons "act something like a neural Wi-Fi to connect with another brain."[2] We see the possibility of such connections in comments from participants such as, "Although the Talent Catalyst only reflected what I said, I gained new insights and ideas that I didn't have before. I don't think that I would have come up with those ideas if I had just sat there thinking by myself." We invite you to observe these possibilities in your Talent Catalyst Conversations.

Gives You Freedom to Be in Charge

Remember, if you are the Talent Catalyst, this Conversation is not about you. If you have a good connection with the participant, perhaps he or she will be a good Talent Catalyst for you too. The Talent Catalyst's role is to help the participant rise to action and achieve some encouraging outcomes. The Talent Catalyst is not looking for a particular result. The Talent Catalyst has enormous freedom to be present and supportive, while freeing the participant from worrying about the Talent Catalyst's expectations of him or her.

HOW A CATALYST DIFFERS FROM A MENTOR OR A COACH

You might wonder: How does the role of Talent Catalyst differ from being a mentor or coach? While there are varying definitions for *mentor* and *coach*, we can distinguish the role of Talent Catalyst along several dimensions.

A mentor is there to pass on his or her knowledge about a career and the way that he or she succeeded in it. The mentor takes an approach of "Learn from me—see how I did it—and you can follow."

A coach is there to inspire someone and champion him or her for some period of time in a more open way than the mentor uses. Unlike the mentor, who aims to pass on knowledge, the coach aims to help a person mine his or her own knowledge and resources. The coach is present to open up possibilities for the other person. But the coach not only is present as the inspiration happens and the train starts moving down the track (as is the case for the Talent Catalyst) but also stays on while the person lays down new track or clears out obstacles as they arise. A coach may play a more multidimensional role than the Catalyst and, of course, serves as a professional with many hours of training and hands-on experience.

In contrast to a coach, the Talent Catalyst needs only to be a willing partner, ask a scripted set of questions, listen generously, and let the participant remain in charge. Because the Catalyst follows a script, it's a role that's relatively easy to start playing. The role of the Catalyst is to stimulate a response and enable the participant to precipitate some desired action and forward progress. See figure 1 for additional discussion of these distinctions.

Of course, after a Talent Catalyst Conversation, the participant might seek a mentor or coach for specific knowledge, help, or more in-depth support. The important point is that the Conversation engages the participant to move as far forward as possible with his or her thinking, and that his or her own deepest hopes and aspirations drive that effort.

If you are in the role of the participant, you may wonder, "Why wouldn't the Talent Catalyst have an ongoing role in my progress?" The simple answer is that you may not need more than the Conversation with the Talent Catalyst. If we create an expectation of an ongoing commitment, it might be awkward for either or both of you. Worse, a bigger commitment could limit whom you might tap for a Talent Catalyst because the

Figure 1. Distinctions between mentor, coach, and talent catalyst.

MENTOR	COACH	TALENT CATALYST
Philosophy or implicit assumptions		
Participants want or need to learn how to do things the way the mentor has done them (guild model).	People with training and skill can support participants in what they want to accomplish.	Participants can take charge of their talent; Catalyst helps them discover their own paths.
Knowledge or training		
Expert in field with clearly demonstrated abilities.	Depth of training in questioning, skilled listening, client focus.	Learn by doing with the Talent Catalyst Conversation Guide and examples.
Relationship with participant		
Top of the field instructing up and comer.	Outside perspective providing professional service.	No special relationship required.
Personal mind-set		
I'm responsible for the participant's well-being.	This is my profession.	I can provide value and have fun without worrying.
Availability		
Limited to experts willing to participate.	Dependent on number of coaches trained.	Any person willing to follow the Talent Catalyst guidelines.

requirements would rise and the matchmaking effort would increase. Then this valuable experience would become more limited and cumbersome. More important, successful Talent Catalyst Conversations frequently identify other people who might be of greater assistance to you in achieving your goals. They become members of your Talent Fulfillment Team. Thus, you're not left on your own. Finally, if an ongoing point of connection makes sense, the desirability of that will bubble up in the Conversation. After all, this is about *you* taking charge of your talent.

WILL THE TALENT CATALYST NEED EXTENSIVE TRAINING?

We've designed the Talent Catalyst Conversation Guide with carefully structured questions for the Talent Catalyst to follow. The structure of the Conversation tracks the framework of the hero's story—hopes, opportunities, and actions. Thus, as you respond to the questions, you'll be dictating an outline of your talent story with you as hero. The Talent Catalyst will take notes for you so that you don't need to interrupt the flow of your thoughts.

In essence, the structured questions take the place of extensive training for the Talent Catalyst. They keep you on track with your better thinking and enable you to win even with a Talent Catalyst who has less experience or training than you.

HOW TO PICK A TALENT CATALYST

The beauty of the Talent Catalyst role is that anyone who is willing to embody the four attributes described above can play it. It could be your spouse, friend, coworker, boss, or employee. Two colleagues can choose to step out to a restaurant and be Talent Catalysts for one another during their lunch break. A manager can put on the Catalyst hat and engage her team members, or an employee can be a Talent Catalyst for his manager. The IT director can spend some time serving as Catalyst for the HR director. This works with any combination you can imagine. As your Talent Catalyst Conversation will last only about an hour, you don't need to fret over who will play the role of your Talent Catalyst. You can always choose a different Talent Catalyst for a future Conversation if you wish.

Seek someone with whom you feel comfortable and who can engage in the Talent Catalyst role without pressing his or her own agenda. If your spouse is worried about money, and you want to quit your job and start a new business, he or she may not be the best person to have the Conversation with. The role of the Talent Catalyst during the Conversation will be to support you and your hopes, not the Talent Catalyst's hopes or those of the organization (although they often intersect). With this flexibility and ease, barriers break down and a culture of talent development starts to grow.

The structure of the Talent Catalyst script provides a "plug and play" formula into which you can bring any willing partner. You can seek out an acquaintance or work with the convenient partner who is before you. Over the years, this open model has led to amazing matchups and successful results. For example, the CEO of an organization had a front-line employee serve as his Talent Catalyst. As it happened, the CEO's hopes focused on how to engage employees more deeply in the organization's work. The front-line employee thoughtfully followed the Talent Catalyst Conversation Guide, and the CEO identified some specific actions to boost employee engagement. Of course, the CEO couldn't have had a better way to demonstrate his intent than to have a front-line employee serve as his Talent Catalyst.

HOW THE CATALYST CAN OFFER IDEAS WITHOUT TAKING AWAY YOUR POWER

What if you don't have ready answers to the questions about resources, opportunities, or actions and the Catalyst has ideas? Can the Catalyst offer them? Yes, but the Catalyst needs to do so carefully. As noted in the Talent Catalyst Conversation Guide, the Catalyst can ask you if you'd like to hear some ideas or if you'd like to brainstorm together. If you feel comfortable receiving them, say yes. If, however, you are doing well or want to stick with your own ideas, gracefully decline. A critical success factor for the Conversation is that you remain in charge and own the results. Otherwise, how can you be the hero of your story? You'll just be a character in someone else's story about your talent.

COULDN'T YOU SIMPLY DO IT ON YOUR OWN?

You could read the questions in the Talent Catalyst Conversation Guide and write in your answers on your own. Do-it-yourselfers report the following benefits:

> It prompted me to think about questions I hadn't considered.

> I feel clearer about my situation and possible opportunities.

> I'm beginning to see a path for myself.

Those participants describe that they made "some progress" and rate the experience as "high value"—that is, excellent return for the limited effort.

Participants often gain transformative results, however, when they connect with a Talent Catalyst, who can provide a unique mirror for them to see themselves from a fresh perspective. Participants who pursue this route frequently report "major progress." People who have worked with the questions on their own and felt their answers were flat comment that the Conversation with the Talent Catalyst enlivened their thinking and yielded a deeper engagement with what was important to them and what they wanted to do.

Here are some of the specific benefits that participants describe from their experiences with a Talent Catalyst.

> It helped to say what I was thinking to get my ideas sorted out and clarified.

> New insights and ideas opened up for me because I felt the Talent Catalyst really listened to me and took a strong interest in my success.

I appreciated the perspectives that the Talent Catalyst added to my thinking when I asked for them.

Speaking my ideas helped me to overcome the writer's block and self-judgment that creep in when I just sit by myself with questions like these.

When I expressed my ideas and intended actions to my Talent Catalyst, they became more real to me. I felt more engaged and committed.

Other people in my life have agendas or expectations for me. In contrast, my Talent Catalyst (at least for this conversation) stayed in my corner, just focused on supporting me, and didn't try to drive me anywhere.

Whether you are skeptical or enthusiastic about the value of a Talent Catalyst Conversation, the only way to know for sure is to try one. We invite you to find a Talent Catalyst or be a Talent Catalyst for someone else, and experience it from that perspective.

WHAT ARE THE BENEFITS FOR THE TALENT CATALYST?

Why would someone be willing to be a Talent Catalyst for you? Many people want to help others to use their talent and find fulfillment. They just don't know how. Here are some of the comments we hear:

"I'd like to help other people, but I don't want to interfere or, worse, feel responsible for what may happen."

"I'm not familiar with the details of their situations, so I worry that I might tell them the wrong thing to do."

"These younger generations have a whole new way of doing things. I'm not sure that my ideas apply or would even be welcome."

You've learned enough about the Talent Catalyst role to know that it avoids all these pitfalls. Talent Catalysts aren't answer providers (although they may provide relevant perspectives, if they have them and the participant asks for them). Talent Catalysts don't need to know the participants' particular circumstances in order to ask the questions, reflect effectively, and encourage the participants' forward action. You'll find people eager to be a Talent Catalyst for you, especially when they understand how simple and straightforward it is and that the formal commitment is only for a one-hour Conversation.

A TALENT CATALYST IN ACTION

Let's return to Fran and see the difference that a Talent Catalyst and Conversation made for her. Following the Talent Catalyst Conversation Guide, her Talent Catalyst didn't get sidetracked by challenging Fran's thinking, as her friend Jules did. Instead, he went to the core of her motivation with the questions "What are your hopes?" and "Why are they important to you?" These reconnected Fran with where she wanted to go, not with what her story had been. With her forward thinking engaged, she identified her success stories for how she had found step-by-step ways to work through challenges and accomplish seemingly unachievable objectives, such as getting a master's degree while working full time and fulfilling her role as a mother in a young family.

Fran's Talent Catalyst sparked a big leap for her by asking Fran how she might start demonstrating her supervisory skills immediately. Based on answers to the prior questions, Fran thought about her hopes, past successes, and resources and outlined actions she could take to begin behaving like a supervisor in the projects she coordinated. Of course, she needed to gain support from others to do that. The important thing was that she took charge of her talent and moved forward. You can read

Fran's Talent Catalyst Conversation and the summary notes that her Talent Catalyst took for her in the "Resources" section.

We'll return to Fran in Keys #2 and #3 to show how she put her plan together and made it a winning situation for her and her organization. For now, the message is that even seemingly impossible stories can change for the good. You just need a catalyst to get them started.

TALENT TAKEAWAY

A Talent Catalyst is a fresh and relatively easy and fun role for people to play. The clear guidelines and structured questions make it something that virtually any willing person can do. Don't let the ease discount its value, however. The Talent Catalyst gets to practice generous listening and asking open-ended questions. Many people find these skills valuable not only at work but also at home and in other dimensions of their lives. Enjoy exploring the possibilities.

TAKE CHARGE

Who will be your Talent Catalyst? Here's a simple checklist to help you determine whom you would like to ask: (1) willing partner, (2) agrees to follow the structured questions, (3) able to be a generous listener, and (4) will allow you to stay in charge without a preconceived idea of the Conversation's outcome. If someone satisfies all four criteria, that person clearly is a match for you. If the person fits two or fewer, he or she probably isn't a match. But don't be a perfectionist here. Some people you know may be more than willing to shift their behaviors in order to be of service to you in the Conversation. Ask someone to be your Talent Catalyst and enjoy the Conversation. Think of it as an invitation to a party in your honor—honoring you as the hero of your story. The door is open. We invite you to enter.

One of the biggest obstacles to progress is a lack of follow-through. Key #2 addresses the most frequent causes: difficulty of sustaining focus, limited resources, and lack of time to accomplish the targeted actions. Whether you've achieved a breakthrough in your Talent Catalyst Conversation or feel that something is still in your way, you will find helpful tools to put your talent fully in play.

Key #2

ACCELERATE THROUGH OBSTACLES

Keep Your Hopes Humming **+** Grab Opportunities to Grow **+** Challenge Yourself to Stretch **=** **Accelerate through Obstacles**

Your Talent Catalyst Conversation may have helped to energize a new chapter in your talent story. That's great! It's as though you've started the ignition in a new car, and you're ready to put it in gear. Your hopes are a scenic highway. Bon voyage!

What are you waiting for? Are you concerned that there will be obstacles in your way? Of course there will be. If you're driving from New York to Los Angeles, you can't wait for all the lights to turn green before you start. You need to turn your talent loose with room to run. It needs to find the right combination of practices to keep it freely flowing. This involves a mix of both playful exercises to sustain innovative thinking and linear methods to transform ideas into action. Thus, this key addresses both the *being* and the *doing* of your talent development—how you think and how you act. We provide concrete guidance so that you can put the ideas in play for yourself.

So what about those obstacles—the breakdowns of hope, the traffic jams of time and commitments, and the one-way streets of opportunity? Do you have the determination and enthusiasm to keep moving forward? How can you tap available people and resources to support your progress? Can you find new ways to stretch and improve your performance? This key helps you to navigate such questions. We encourage you to use these obstacles to sharpen your skills, learn, create, and grow while inspiring yourself and the world around you. This is not the time to slow down or fall into old habits of limited thinking and comfortable lethargy. It is the time to move forward with alacrity: brisk and cheerful readiness.

We encourage you to try all the exercises, especially the ones that seem unfamiliar or, dare we say, irrelevant to you. New surprises may await you. Don't just read about the exercises. That's like looking at a buffet but never tasting anything. Try the exercises. They all can serve you as you take charge of your talent. After sampling, you can pick those practices you'd like to add to your regular diet. You'll know that you've found the right combination when your talent engages your interest, energy, and commitment to express it.

Chapter 4

KEEP YOUR HOPES HUMMING

Optimism is the faith that leads to achievement. Nothing can be done without hope or confidence.

HELEN KELLER

When your hopes are alive and flourishing, you naturally move forward with confidence. As the hero of your own story, you'll need to stay focused to sustain yourself on the journey into the territory of new possibilities. Learning how to live in a cycle of hope will not only energize you and keep you committed but also support your best creative thinking, which is imperative to your success.

You've opened the door for your talent. Let's nourish it to thrive.

CHOOSE YOUR HOPES OVER FEARS

Have you noticed that some days you feel creative and open to new ideas and opportunities and other days you don't? We see it all the time. People who are no smarter or more experienced successfully launch themselves forward, while others just see insurmountable obstacles in every direction. The way we respond to our environment is all related to how our brains are wired and which pathways we choose to follow on our journeys.

Do you remember Fran? All the jobs she wanted seemed to have a big "No Entrance!" sign. Fran wanted to become a manager. She didn't have the prerequisites. "I don't think I'm going to make progress anytime soon," she said before her Talent Catalyst Conversation. During the Conversation, she realized that she had resources all around her that she had never noticed. With this new awareness, she created an action plan to move toward her hope. It was a turning point for her.

At first, Fran enjoyed a rush of excitement in knowing that her story could change. When she returned to her daily work, however, old thought patterns cropped up. "I don't know if I can pull this off. I'd be really putting myself out there to enlist the CEO and others to help me. What if my efforts crash and burn?" Feeling uneasy, she left the summary of her Conversation turned upside down under a potted plant on her desk. Just as Superman lost his power when he got too close to kryptonite, Fran lost her power when she got too close to her fears of failure and inadequacy.

Different parts of the brain serve different purposes. Human brains function for both self-protection and creation. Given the same challenging situation, two people may respond very differently: one person may see the possibilities and forge ahead, while another holds tight to what feels safe. Science shows that your frame of mind plays a major role in the opportunities you see and the possibilities you pursue. Fear-based thinking shuts down the creative centers of your brain, but hope-based thinking ignites them. Just when Fran felt inspired to move forward, her worst fears arose. We'll explore what she did, and what you can do, to break the cycle of fear.

Fears Block Your Best Thinking

While fears stimulate a protective response that serves a valuable purpose when encountering physical threats, that response can wreak havoc with your creativity. Think about the last time you felt threatened. How did your body react? If a cobra hovers around your ankle and you're overcome with heart palpitations, you most likely won't be working out the last lines of your best-selling novel. Your brain is in full-throttle protection mode. Although it may not seem as dramatic, the very same thing can happen when you feel threatened by a problem at work. Your brain may go into the same reactive mode, diverting energy from the regions that handle complex creative issues and undercutting your access to original solutions just when you need them most.

David Rock, in *Your Brain at Work*, explains: "When the limbic system gets overly aroused, it reduces the resources available for prefrontal cortex functions [including understanding, deciding, memorizing, and inhibiting]. ... With less glucose and oxygen to get work done, the complex maps in your prefrontal cortex required for conscious processes don't function as they should."[1]

Let's get back to Fran. Just when she needed access to new and creative ways to overcome the challenges in her career, her limbic brain took over. The problem was that she wasn't deciding whether to fight a tiger or run for her life. She really didn't need that primal fear response to kick into action. Instead, she needed the creative parts of her brain engaged, but they were losing power. Fear and frustration hijacked her better thinking.

Fear blinds us to possibilities and paralyzes us all at once. Even worse, we may take self-protective measures when we're afraid, which in turn bring to life the very thing we feared would occur in the first place. Maybe you've been in this rut and felt yourself dragged down as you went deeper and deeper.

Fran was in a vicious cycle of fear (see figure 2). She felt a deadening sense of discouragement and didn't feel the momentum to get into the game. Her withdrawal further distanced her from the flow of opportunities that could change her story. Like Fran, most of us have fallen prey to this vicious cycle of fear. We have felt our minds looping around and around, telling us a repetitive story of doom, making us want to run for our lives or fight to protect our stand. When we're in a fearful or self-protective mode, we're not usually much fun. We may blame others, find it hard to listen, and become reactive. Our bodies may

Figure 2. Vicious cycle of fear.

tense up, stomachs grind, or heads start to throb from the stress. Fear can make us sick, crabby, tired, and depressed.

The good news is that when we become aware of our reactions and realize that we are stuck in a fear cycle, we can choose a different response. The first step back into a healthier frame of mind is becoming aware.

Your Hopes Encourage Creative, Constructive Thinking

While a cycle of fear can sometimes give you a burst of energy to get things done, the wear and tear on your body and mind is rarely worth it. Making a conscious choice to keep connected to your hopes allows you to walk a self-sustaining path of talent expression. When you are hopeful, your creative brain is lit up and supporting all your decisions.

Shawn Achor, founder of Good Think, Inc., and author of *The Happiness Advantage*, writes: "Our brains are literally hardwired to perform at their best not when they are negative or even neutral, but when they are positive. Yet in today's world, we ironically sacrifice happiness in order to excel in the workforce only to lower our brains' success rates."[2] By staying hopeful, we shift our brains' activity to support the thinking we need for sustained, creative action. *It's that simple.* This virtuous cycle

Figure 3. Virtuous cycle of hope.

Hopes

Opportunities

Actions

of hope gives us a sense of possibility that opens our minds to the resources all around us. It becomes easier to identify emerging opportunities and take the actions to move toward what we desire. Figure 3 illustrates this positive cycle.

This cycle is also self-reinforcing, but in a positive way. When we are hopeful, we see more opportunities and take actions that are more constructive. As we see our hopes come to fruition, we naturally choose to continue to reach out to others and pursue more resources and actions.

Have you ever experienced the feeling of being full of hope? When we are overflowing with hope, one good thing leads to another. We look for opportunities, and our actions become self-fulfilling. When hope is on the loose, we interact with others more thoughtfully and feel less edgy overall. Our bodies function more smoothly, and we get sick less often. If we hit a bump, we keep going and stay focused. The world looks friendlier, and our eyes are open to the resources around us.

Since a hopeful frame of mind has such clear advantages, how can you train yourself to consistently choose it? You took the first step in your Talent Catalyst Conversation when you answered the questions "What are your hopes?" and "Why are they important to you?" By answering these simple, open-ended questions, you triggered the creative and problem-solving centers of your brain. You can do this over and over again wherever you are and whatever you confront. Stop and ask yourself: "What do I really want here? Which frame of mind will help me?" Knowing that you have a choice in deciding your frame of mind puts you in charge.

NURTURE YOUR HOPES — THREE EASY WAYS

Since our brains have a default setting for a fearful or protective response, we need conscious action to override it. The following practices will support your hopeful frame of mind and productive results.

Take 5

"Take 5" is the practice of spending five minutes a day giving focused attention to your hopes for your talent. Without consistent attention, your hopes can become lost in the hubbub of daily life, other people's agendas, and fearful thoughts that emanate from the media and other sources. You can use these five minutes to recognize a daily victory, contemplate the significant value of your hope, or visualize something to realize it.

Consider Take 5 to be an exercise in developing a good habit. You might want to put it on your calendar or include it as part of your morning routine. Some people enjoy doing it as a writing or drawing exercise; others prefer it as a meditation. Take 5 can involve both your *conscious* and *unconscious mind,* which may be holding on to some important details related to your hopes that you can uncover only when disengaged from your day-to-day activities.

We invite you to schedule Take 5 sessions for a week and see how they work for you. For example, you could take a few minutes in the morning to outline some steps you intend to take in the day to help realize your hopes. Later in the day, you might review how your actions during the past few hours fulfilled those intentions. Keep notes on the progress you see toward your hopes. As you give yourself positive feedback on what's working, you will reinforce and accelerate your success.

Of course, not everything will occur in an unendingly positive direction. Concerns will crop up as you reflect on your hopes. When they do, simply acknowledge them and return to considering your hopes. On some days, you may fulfill more than you had targeted on the items you jotted down. On other days, circumstances may intervene, and you may fulfill fewer of your intentions than you had planned. Observe what's happening for you with compassionate self-interest. The practice of thoughtful attention will engage your mind in the direction you seek.

Make Your Hopes Visible

One of the challenges you may face is staying fully—even physically—connected to your hopes over the long haul. In a world with so many responsibilities, messages, and priorities, you need to give your brain some prompts to stay engaged.

Imagine that your hope is to learn how to play the banjo. Do you think you would be more likely to play and practice regularly if you kept the banjo in the closet or out in the open where you saw it daily?

One of the best ways to get your hopes out of the closet is to give them physical form. Create a symbolic representation that will, metaphorically, wave its arms to remind you of why your hopes are important to you or poke you whenever you start getting off track.

Here are just a few of the solutions we've found people using that worked for them and might also work for you:

> A collage of all the rewards you'll get when your hope is realized

A collage of all the resources you plan to use to realize your hopes

A nametag or business card with your desired new job title

A totem or memory-rich object given to you by someone special

A screen saver with phrases or pictures that inspire you

A subscription to a blog or newsletter that regularly sends you articles that motivate you to stay on track

Group meetings or classes that keep you engaged in putting your specific hopes into action

A "gold star" system in which you collect small rewards as you take steps forward, like making a date to see a great movie with a friend once you have accomplished a goal

What kind of real-world reminder would work best for you? How about getting started by putting one in place today?

Have Your Very Own Hope Holders

Think of your hopes for your talent as a flame. You want to keep the flame glowing brightly, yet it's easy for any of us to have ups and downs that dim our fire. A Hope Holder is a person whose main job is to champion your hope: to remind you of how it sprang forth, how good it makes you feel, and why it remains valuable today. You may want to include a Hope Holder on your Talent Fulfillment Team. Hope Holders are like the crowds that line the streets of a marathon, cheering on the runners when they need it most.

We found mutual hope holding invaluable as we wrote this book. When one of us would be discouraged or distracted, the other would hold the hope and keep things moving forward.

You want Hope Holders who are dedicated to being there

for you through thick and thin: *as if your hope were a sacred trust*. Of course you're not limited to having just one Hope Holder. The secret is to choose wisely. Sometimes our friends have their own agendas that don't fit with the role, or they want to tend to us rather than tend the flame. Out of all your friends and family, maybe someone is coming to mind as a good Hope Holder. Remember, before he or she can hold your vision for you, you have to be clear about what your hope is. Maybe now would be a good time to share your hope with another and ask him or her to hold your hope in mind.

Fran put all three practices to work as she moved away from her fears and kept her talent story powered up. She remembered her Talent Catalyst Conversation and the image she had of her Talent Fulfillment Team cheering for her as she led a team to successful results. She got pictures of each of them and kept that image on her desk. It reminded her of what she really wanted and encouraged her as she took the many actions needed to realize her aspirations. This became the focal point for her Take 5 daily reflections.

TURN CONCERNS INTO ENERGIZERS

You'll recall the discussion in the Talent Catalyst Conversation Guide about concerns:

> *When we focus on our deepest hopes, our brains often attempt to protect us from harm by generating stories of concern. Ignoring them could be dangerous; yet assuming they can't be overcome will also limit what is possible. For now, we suggest that you simply acknowledge their presence.*

It's time now to do more than consider the presence of your concerns. We'll look more deeply to see if it's possible to use them to stimulate your talent—not suppress it.

Get Your *But* Out of the Way

It's not unusual to discover that people who are not using all their talents have a big BUT. OK—bad joke, but it's true. That big *but* can block the path to achieving hopes. Do you remember Ben, the teacher we talked about in chapter 2? Let's take a look at Ben's story from another angle. In chapter 2, we talked about how he used his talent to help disadvantaged kids through after-school programming and how this got his energy flowing again. Now, we'll look at how he managed to get his *but*s out of the way right in his own classroom.

Ben told us: "As a high school teacher, my hope has always been to get kids to love learning, *but* I still feel I'm at the mercy of the bureaucracy. I want to teach and show the kids that learning is great, *but* how can I do that with all of the regulations and tests?"

In this case, the big *but* concerned regulations and standardized tests—pretty common concerns for teachers. His concerns—what he felt blocked him—interfered with his hope to show the kids that learning is great. When concerns occur as interference, they can slow you down, bring you to a halt, or even throw you off-track completely. Concerns gone wild not only smother your ability to bring a single hope to fulfillment but also destroy your overall belief in your talent.

Let's take a look at Ben's original desire: "My hope has always been to get kids to love learning." As Ben explained, "The regulations and policies are hard to work around and seriously frustrating. I don't want to teach to a test; the learning loses its meaning. I want the kids to feel that what they are learning will help them now and enrich the rest of their lives, not just get them into the next grade or through high school. I don't want to teach them to be trained monkeys, always doing something to get a payoff. I think the real payoff for education is that your life is richer, and I want my students to inherit that from me."

After looking at his concerns, Ben realized he still had so

much resistance to the system that he had created a larger-than-life mental block that drove him to consider giving up on classroom teaching altogether. How could he break through the logjam?

Ben began thinking about what action he could take that would make even one of his classes feel livelier and fun. He went back through some books from grad school and looked up interactive teaching ideas on the Internet. He also spoke with his wife, an outstanding English teacher.

The next week, Ben started fresh. He talked with the students about his hopes and asked them for their ideas. They had a brainstorming session in each class and came up with some great suggestions. He commented, "My classes flew by, just like the old days when I first started teaching. We were learning the same material, but I was able to present it in a way that the kids got really engaged. Now I just have to figure out how to keep it going for the long run—and I can tell you honestly, that won't be easy, but I'm seeing some light." Ben was beginning to overcome what had interfered with his hopes.

Timothy Gallwey, author of the *Inner Game* series, uses an interesting approach to help athletes and businesspeople get the most from their talent. Rather than having people try harder or try to do things correctly, he suggests that they identify what is interfering with their performance and simply remove it.[3] For example, a writing coach might help a client to "kill the editor" in order to free the writer's productivity. The editor is that nagging voice in a writer's head that whispers, "You aren't smart enough to write anything worth reading." Many internal editors have been the demise of otherwise talented writers. By outsmarting their own brains with the use of exercises, writers can learn to write without editing themselves simultaneously. They "put the editor to bed" for a while, and this often brings energy and inspiration to their words.

Interference can be subtle and hard to identify. Many of our concerns may seem logical on the surface. However, they often signify subterranean limiting assumptions and beliefs we hold that we may not know we possess.

It's good to remember that concerns are the brain's way of protecting us. Therefore, it can be important to attend to those thoughts — for example:

> "I really want to suggest a new idea for improving communications around the office, *but* I might get fired if I do."

> "I would love to take a class in website design, *but* I couldn't possibly leave the office at 4 p.m. on Thursdays."

> "My dream is to make partner, *but* I'll never be able to put in the hours needed, due to the demands of my family life."

Do you have a big *but?* If so, take a moment to examine it and see if you can unchain yourself. Will you really get fired? Are you sure you can't get buy-in for professional development? Is it certain that your family life has to come at the expense of your job promotion? If your concerns are blocking the full expression of your talent, it could be useful to inquire into the limiting assumption or belief upon which those concerns are based.

Eliminating the interference that is preventing you from accessing and expressing your full talent can create an everyone-wins situation for you, your organization, and the people in your workplace, family, and community.

Flip Your Concerns into Hopes

Here is another perspective to give you a boost when your concerns are slowing you down. Did you ever accidentally put a CD in your stereo upside down? Nothing happens, right? But when you turn it to the flip side, music starts to play. What if your concerns are just the flip side of your hopes?

Instead of accepting concerns at face value—as obstacles—consider examining them more closely so that they become guideposts to what you really want. If you have a concern, after all, it means you care about something. In that caring you can find your hopes!

For instance, consider Nadia's situation in a large health care organization struggling to adapt to major changes in its industry. She commented: "My goal has been, and still is, to accelerate change in the entire organization. That's the job they asked me to do. I received a promotion and an assignment, and I took it seriously."

Nadia certainly set out to drive toward her objective. But she did so at some cost to herself. Anyone who wasn't "with the program" became an obstacle. She started to judge many coworkers as insubordinate or incompetent. Perhaps it wasn't a coincidence that she developed severe digestive problems. She felt that she was failing. "My chief concerns are that I've alienated some important people, and now they do their best to undermine my efforts."

So what happened when she looked at the flip side of her concerns?

> The flip side of "I've alienated important people" was "I want to have healthy, productive relationships."

> The flip side of "Now they do their best to undermine my efforts" was "I want to be supported in my efforts to accelerate change."

It wasn't hard for Nadia to see that this flip side was actually her deeper hope. This turned out to be quite an emotional moment for her. It even moved her to tears. She realized that although she thought of herself as a truly caring person, she had stopped caring about the people working with her. She had tried so hard to push the change initiative forward—thinking only of pleasing her superiors—that she submerged one of her greatest talents: her compassion. Unwittingly she had become the villain in her story instead of the hero.

How did Nadia articulate her hope now? "My hope is to help

people see how embracing change can make their lives richer, while making the entire organization more competitive in the marketplace."

Almost immediately, things began to shift. She felt a great reduction in her stress level, and her health began to improve. Three months after her internal decision to shift toward acting from the realm of her hope instead of coercing her coworkers out of her fear of failure, she received a call from a vice president. He had originally been the most resistant and undermining out of all the staff. He called to apologize for his behavior and asked to start a dialogue that would get them on the same page.

Nadia used the flip-side approach to get in touch with a genuine hope. This hope helped her to recast herself as the hero of her story and to tap a dormant talent.

Like Nadia, if you are willing to see the hope in your concern, you can begin to move from fear and worry to a healthy vision you can act upon. Take a minute or two to jot down your answers to these questions:

What are the flip sides of your concerns?

What are your hopes now that you have flipped your concerns around?

Through this process of recasting your concerns into hopes, you can return to the realm of possibility: a place where you can use your talent to create the reality that you want to live.

Craft an Inspirational Story with Yourself in the Lead

You can use your hopes to write new chapters in your talent story. Think back to the question in the Talent Catalyst Conversation that asked, "How have you successfully dealt with concerns like these before?" (step 3). This question gets at the stories we tell about ourselves and helps us to recall how we have managed to deal with fears and problems in the past. Can you find a story from your past that gives you a vision for pursuing your hopes now? To engage your talent fully, you must have a way to step outside of limiting stories and explore what else may be possible. Let's look at a couple of ways you can gain fresh perspectives and author the stories you want to live by—stories that engage your talent.

Robert Hargrove, in his book *Masterful Coaching*, makes the distinction between "rut stories" and "river stories."[4] Rut stories keep us stuck in a paradigm of limitation; river stories are filled with possibility because they have somewhere to flow. Nadia just showed us one way to move from rut to river by discovering the hopes on the flip side of her concerns. But rut stories are not just about being stuck. Nadia's story also demonstrated how much pain a rut story can inflict on the storyteller and those around her.

Let's look at an illustration of how you can change your story. Miguel, a senior manager in a large IT firm, saw opportunities but worried about the human cost of going to the top.

I have much more that I could contribute to the organization, but rising higher in the leadership would compromise time with my family and require me to be too political. I'll keep my head down and continue plugging away at my current role. I guess it's better to be a little bored.

Now, think of what he honestly shared as not the *truth* but a *story*. Here are the "facts" as he presents them:

1. I have much more that I could contribute to the organization. (*hope story*)

2. Rising higher in the leadership would compromise time with my family and require me to be too political. (*story of concern*)

3. I guess it's better to be a little bored. (*rut story*)

4. I'll keep my head down and continue plugging away at my current role. (*limited action plan*)

Clearly none of the thoughts Miguel shared are facts in the same way that 2 + 2 = 4 is a fact. They are all interpretations. His limited action plan ("keep my head down and continue plugging away") is perfectly logical, given the story he has told. Yet his action plan does not move him toward the realization of his hopes. His story does not support him realizing his hopes because it is a rut story. His talents are not engaged; they are submerged.

What could Miguel do with his rut story about how a promotion would mean compromising his family values and require him to be too political? Miguel, as it happens with many people, had trouble coming up with any previous successes to allay his particular concerns. Notice how his concern is the more powerful driver in his story—not his hope. What about inventing an altogether new, more powerful story?

What would it be like for Miguel to retell his story about a possible promotion? Here's one possibility (that actually happened):

1. I have much more that I could contribute to the organization. In fact, this organization really needs what I have to offer. (*story of hope*)

2. Rising higher in the leadership could compromise time with my family and require me to be too political. (*story of concern*)

3. I'm not willing to let that happen. I will find a way to make sure that doesn't happen. (*river story*)

4. I'll identify some people who have been promoted and who have succeeded at staying real and honest while balancing their work and business lives. I'll ask one of them to guide me. (*new action plan*)

Are your concerns driving your story as they were originally for Miguel, or are your hopes leading the way? You get to author your own inspirational story. What will it take for you to change your story for the better?

One way would be to examine your story from different perspectives. Seeing through other people's eyes can help you to see hope where before there was concern. Go back to Miguel's story, this time checking on the different perspectives from people in his life. If Miguel were to ask his boss, wife, kids, and most supportive friends for their perspectives on his story, what might he hear?

> BOSS: We're glad to have you on board and moving up in management. A mentor sounds like a solid idea, although you'll have to seek that relationship on your own time.

> WIFE: Honey, you know I want you to be happy. Just remember to keep us in mind.

> KIDS: I don't care, Dad—as long as you can make it to some of my games.

> FRIEND: What kind of example are you being for your kids when you settle for something less than you can be?

Of course, these are just some possibilities. If Miguel were to take the time to look from those different perspectives, he might just see things in a different light. How does your story look from a different perspective?

TALENT TAKEAWAY

Our thought patterns drive our results. While ingrained fearful patterns protect us, they also hold us back from taking charge. You can stop the fear cycle and override it by shifting your attention to your hopeful, hero story. This allows you to calm your protective instincts long enough to explore new frontiers. Consciously choosing a hopeful frame of mind and acting to keep your hopes alive provides the necessary motivation to sustain your talent and accelerate results.

TAKE CHARGE

Keep your hopes alive with one or more of these exercises.

Nurture Your Hopes

1. **Take 5.** Spend five minutes a day giving focused attention to your hopes for your talent. Think about what you want to have happen, and note opportunities and progress toward your hopes.

2. **Make your hopes visible.** Create images and reminders in your environment to keep your deepest hopes in mind.

3. **Have your very own Hope Holders.** Ask the right people to tend the flame of your inspiration and never let you give up on yourself.

Turn Concerns into Energizers

1. **Get your *but* out of the way.** Examine how you think about things that get in your way. Remove whatever is interfering with moving toward your hopes, or shift your attention so that you can let your hopes burn more brightly.

2. **Flip your concerns into hopes.** Explore your concerns to see what hope underlies them. They will help you turn to positive outcomes.

3. **Craft an inspirational story with yourself in the lead.** Write a story that describes how you want your hopes to come to fruition. Describe how you will get out of the ruts and make the story flow.

Chapter 5

GRAB OPPORTUNITIES TO GROW

*The pessimist sees difficulty in every opportunity. The optimist sees
the opportunity in every difficulty.*

WINSTON CHURCHILL

To bring your hopes home, you will have to keep a vigilant
watch and grab opportunities that come your way. You've already
developed an eagle's eye to focus on your hopes and transform
many seemingly dead-end situations into beneficial pathways. In
this chapter, we will look at three core ways of *being* and *doing*
that will help you to express your talent and realize your hopes.
Let's have a preview.

> **Be open to opportunities.** Does this sound too simple? You will
> be surprised at how many opportunities you miss simply
> because you don't notice them. When you look at the world
> with fresh eyes, you will see what you did not see before.

> **Develop the inner qualities that will help you get to where you want to
> go.** You'll see which qualities serve you best, which qualities
> you may wish to enhance, and which qualities you may like
> to engage in others to bring your talent into its fullest power.

> **Expand your use of resources to help you move forward.** We have all
> felt, "I just don't have the resources to accomplish what I
> want." Accessing resources is a lot easier than it may appear,
> and we will guide you to find the precise resources you
> need to make things happen.

BE OPEN TO OPPORTUNITIES

Everyone likes to look good and feel that he or she is on top of his or her game. Having confidence is a sign of a healthy ego and strong self-esteem. To grow, though, we also need to reach out and acknowledge what we don't know, explore new ideas, and try mastering new skills. This isn't a simple, effortless endeavor. It requires openness.

To understand the importance of openness, let's take a quick look at the research. Carol Dweck, a psychology professor at Stanford University, has spent decades examining what drives people and what determines their achievement levels. In her book *Mindset: The New Psychology of Success*, she concludes that humans have two basic approaches to life.[1] One she calls a "fixed mindset," which views intelligence and talent as preset and finite. When people subscribe to this view, they might say, "I've got what I've got, and nothing will change." In many respects, they apply the limitations of physical attributes to their talent. "I can't grow taller, so why should I think that I can make significant increases in my talent?"

In contrast, when people have a "growth mindset," they view intelligence and talent as something they can increase. They can learn new ideas, develop new skills, and benefit from watching others who are successful. They aren't stuck. They can change their talent story through mastery of new areas.

Let's look at these different views as they relate to opportunities to grow your talent. Figure 4 provides our interpretation of the contrasts between a fixed mind-set and a growth mind-set as they relate to talent.

Which frame of mind describes your predominant outlook about your talent at this time? Maybe you are in the middle—holding some beliefs as fixed and others as growth. Can you recognize yourself anywhere in figure 4?

If you have adopted the belief, as part of a fixed view about

Figure 4. Contrasting mind-sets about talent.

Fixed	Growth
You see your talent and abilities as fixed.	You look at yourself as a work in progress rather than a finished product.
Your eagerness to prove yourself overwhelms your willingness to learn.	Your "beginner's mind" serves as a powerful engine for inquiry rather than a sign of your ignorance.
You seek effortless success with the skills and abilities you have.	You see your talent as an abundant resource rather than a predetermined set of strengths.
You tend to think everything is about the immediate outcome.	Your hopes are a guide to long-term growth and fulfillment.

your talent, that you can't do certain things, that you are not worthy of aspiring to some better opportunity, or that you are incapable, you are not very likely to see the universe as a place with abundant opportunities.

On the other hand, even if you feel that you are a long way off from where you want to be in expressing your talent, when you have an open mind about your abilities, you have the impetus to learn and move forward.

In an organization whose leadership exhibits a dominant fixed mind-set, people in lower-level jobs are destined to stay there and are rarely consulted for their opinions or contributions. At the same time, upper levels become so consumed with producing great results in the short term and maintaining image and status that they run the risk of distorting facts or ignoring realities until the organization suffers.

Many of us develop a fixed mind-set because at some point it served a purpose. It may have helped us to make sense of the world, helped us to get important needs met, and protected us from perceived threats. However, if you want to take charge of your talent fully, holding on to this worldview will be costly. It will keep you stuck in a story about limitations rather than free you to create a story full of possibilities.

Cultivating openness to growth can strengthen the cycle of hopes, opportunities, and actions in rewarding ways. Anything that engages the brain in learning can open up exciting new and unexpected opportunities. People engaged in growth and learning are more likely not only to achieve success but also to enjoy their success.

What if you discover that you have a fixed mind-set when it comes to your talent? Is it possible to change? Sure it is. When you're ready to find new avenues to express your talent, cultivating openness to growth will help you to cut the path. Let's take a look at Jesse, who shifted his mind-set.

Jesse thought his talent story was set. He'd had a very satisfying career. In his twenty-nine years with the financial services company, he had risen steadily up the ladder to the level of vice president and had found his work pretty easy. Now, at age fifty-eight, he had nowhere to go, unless the senior VP died or retired. As he waited to reach his magic retirement number, he was the envy of many of his friends. But for Jesse the thrill was gone. Every day, he put a smile on his face, did his eight to ten hours, and caught the train back home.

After a routine staff meeting, a young intern approached Jesse and asked if she could have a few minutes of his time. She requested permission to offer a yoga class over the lunch hour. Before he had a chance to respond, she opened her portfolio and pulled out an article about a British study that enumerated the positive effects of exercise at work. The study showed how workday exercise improved job performance and employee engagement while decreasing absenteeism.

The intern's passion about taking on this new initiative moved Jesse. He referred her to the person who could help make it happen.

When Jesse returned to his office, he felt really low. A young, enthusiastic intern had asked to start a new program in her department. She was so full of energy that it caused Jesse to notice his own lack of energy at work. This young intern had her whole career ahead of her, and here he was counting the days until retirement, with little to look forward to. Jesse wasn't sure why all this was hitting him so hard, but it was.

The intern possessed two things that Jesse sorely lacked: openness to growth and enthusiasm. Later, when he thought about where fixed views had blocked his thinking, Jesse laughed. He reflected, "Wow, many areas feel fixed: my role at the office, the idea of retirement, even my political views and my belief that nothing is likely to change."

This was Jesse's *aha!* moment. He realized that it was time to make fresh plans for the next ten years of his life. A new hope arose in him. He kept the intern's article about yoga on his credenza as a reminder of the openness to growth and enthusiasm he wanted to regain.

You can follow the simple recipe that Jesse used to assess your frame of mind and shift from a preset view to openness for growth.

Recipe for Growth

1. **Observe your thought patterns.** In any moment, notice what you are thinking. Are you open to growth at that moment or not? Notice when you have a fixed outlook and things seem unchangeable and stuck. Can you tweak your perspective? How would the same situation look if you were open to change and willing to grow?

2. **Question what feels fixed.** In your current situation, does anything feel fixed? Where do options feel shut off or opportunities feel limited? Now that you have the awareness that

you can find a new perspective, do you see ways to create opportunities or follow leads that may open new doors?

3. **Keep a reminder that inspires you to be open.** What image, object, or experience gives you a sense of openness? Use pictures or actions to remind you. One woman cut out words and phrases from magazines and collected them on a board—words like *shift*, *stretch*, and *go for it*. Another person did the same thing, but with the words trailing across his screen saver. One man kept a photo from his greatest rock climb on his desk. Another woman had an inspiring card her friend had given her in a holder on her desk. Another person set her watch alarm to vibrate every hour, using this to remind herself to check in and see if she was in an open frame of mind.

DEVELOP YOUR INNER QUALITIES — IQS YOU CAN BOOST

Before you leap into action, think about how you want to *be* when you act. Whether you realize it or not, your *being-ness* drives everything you do. That's right. You will go far when you realize this and link the being of talent development with the doing.

The *being* of talent development draws upon your inner qualities—or, as we call them, your *IQs*. Your inner qualities include aspects like curiosity, passion, assertiveness, authenticity, vulnerability, generosity, grace, and respect.

Why are your inner qualities important? They inevitably influence your external actions. For example, think how the expression of different inner qualities would affect the following situations: you address a group of coworkers with passion or hard logic; you approach a conflict with your boss with self-righteousness or compassion; or you attend a training session with vitality or lethargy. As you can imagine, each of the inherent IQs in these scenarios has a profound impact on the results that your actions produce.

Inner qualities are like the rhythm of a song. You need the rhythm to match the melody. If the rhythm is off, it doesn't matter what the melody or message is. The song won't be compelling and captivate others.

Developing your inner qualities will help your talent find its voice. This came through loud and clear in Ranjit's story. Ranjit's Talent Catalyst Conversation began with a focus on his work life, but it soon turned to the subject of his family. His second child was due in a month, and his anxiety was growing daily. He hoped to have a wonderful family life, as well as career, and wanted to be a good husband and father. The truth was, he was already concerned that he was neglecting his wife and spending most of his time focused on his young daughter and work. What was going to happen when a second child appeared? He feared that he'd become sleep deprived and that his daughter would feel neglected. He wasn't sure if he could meet his wife's needs and the demands at work.

Ranjit stepped back and considered what inner qualities he would need to succeed. He looked at how he was *being* at home and what was driving his anxiety; he realized that he was being the "fixer," both at work and at home. Everyone went to him to get things fixed. Suddenly, the lightbulb went on. He was already struggling to fix everything at home—to make sure that everything was working and everyone was happy. With the new baby coming, he was afraid that he would be completely overwhelmed.

Ranjit reviewed the Inner Quality Checklist below to see if he could identify alternative ways of being that would allow him to free up his talent as a father, husband, and employee. Here are the three IQs that resonated for him:

Curiosity

Compassion

Supportiveness

When Ranjit took the time to look these over, he had another realization: "When I'm being the fixer, I'm always looking for things that are broken. I'll stop doing everything else if there's something to fix. I think that's one way my daughter gets my attention. She stirs up trouble, and I fix it. If I were to be curious and compassionate with her, I'd certainly see things differently. And I am really curious to see how my daughter responds. I could go from being the fixer to being the learner—learning from my little daughter and my wife every chance I get. It's exciting to think of what I might see that I didn't see before, and it could be a breath of fresh air for our family."

The more Ranjit practiced at home, the more he found himself embodying those inner qualities at work. When he didn't immediately leap in and try to fix everything for his coworkers, they started to take more responsibility. They also felt more respected by Ranjit because he took an interest in them and their work. The team worked together more effectively. They were singing a new tune together. Ranjit boosted the IQs that really mattered—the inner qualities he needed for success at home and at work.

Now it's your turn. What inner qualities will you need to nurture in order to realize the hopes you have for your talent?

We've put together a list of IQs in six categories for you to consider as you move forward. Remember, this is just an outline. You may want to jot down more qualities that you'd like to add to the list. Here's how we suggest you approach this exercise:

1. Go through the entire list and mark those inner qualities that will be the most important for you to realize your particular hopes at this time.

2. Add any additional qualities to the list that you feel are important to realizing your hopes.

3. While you could mark many, if not all, of the IQs, see if you can identify the three or four that are the most critical for your success.

The Inner Qualities Checklist

Head — Mental Processes

Wise: Use intelligence with a big-picture view

Curious: Approach the world with wonder and the love of learning

Focused: Stay on task and free from distractions

Mindful: Be present to the opportunities at every moment

Heart — Emotional Processes

Compassionate: Recognize and care about others' feelings and needs

Generous: Give and receive freely

Passionate: Care deeply and lovingly about an idea, person, or activity

Vulnerable: Allow others to make a difference to me

Health — Physical Processes

Vital: Feel alive and energetic

Graceful: Dance with difficulties and challenges

Joyful: Appreciate life with a smile on my face

Peaceful: Maintain balance without undue stress

Ingenuity

Creative: Use resources inventively

Inspired: Engage stories, values, and people that move me

Unconventional: Examine limiting assumptions

Visionary: See and communicate possibilities for the future

Relationships

Authentic: Behave in an open and honest manner

Respectful: Treat others as they wish to be treated

Supportive: Actively help others succeed

Gracious: Acknowledge others and accept acknowledgment

Strength

Assertive: Meet my needs without aggression

Courageous: Take action in the face of adversity

Faithful: Remain true to my values

Promotional: Communicate benefits effectively to a community

Other possible IQs might include patient, collaborative, trusting, trustworthy, energized, flexible, light, fun, fresh, playful, serious, attentive, organized, in touch, adult, sober, persistent, and so on.

Once you have identified several important inner qualities, what can you do with them? Some of the critical IQs you've highlighted may already be great strengths and tremendous resources for you. You'll certainly want to use them in your action plan. But what about the inner qualities that you know need more attention and development?

Remember that Ranjit picked three IQs that he wanted to develop: curiosity, compassion, and supportiveness. He wasn't asking himself to be someone he was not. He possessed all of those qualities. He just needed to allow them to come to the fore and make them a priority.

You can access and embody the critical IQs that you need to realize your hopes. Here are some approaches:

Observe and model. Seek out the people who best represent the way you want to be. If you pick "authentic," observe the authentic people you admire and then model the quality for others around you.

Prepare and remind. Before you go into an important meeting, choose the IQ you most want to embody. If you pick "patient," write it on a pad in front of you to keep as a constant reminder.

Learn and practice. For instance, if you want to be more "assertive," read books and articles, watch online videos, or attend workshops on the subject. Then put what you learn into a daily practice to build your assertive character.

Enlist and tap others. If you don't have a sufficient amount of a critical inner quality, enlist others who do. For example, if assertiveness just isn't in your makeup, ask someone to advocate on your behalf.

As you develop and express your critical IQs and enlist others to support them, you will attract more of the opportunities that align with your hopes. It is true that people respond to the way you dress, your physicality, and other external qualities, but they will respond even more powerfully to your IQs. Check out this idea for yourself. Who are the most attractive people in your organization—not necessarily physically attractive but charismatic, admirable, worthy of trust, or in some way fascinating? What do you find attractive about them? How much of what makes them attractive arises from their positive IQs? Do you also notice that when they acknowledge inner qualities where they need help, their candor and vulnerability make them even more attractive?

Consider again one of the questions in the Talent Catalyst Conversation: "How will you need to grow, and what will you need to learn to address your concerns and realize your hopes?" How would you answer that question right now about the inner qualities you wish to strengthen?

EXPAND YOUR RESOURCES, MAXIMIZE YOUR OPPORTUNITIES

Everything any of us has ever accomplished has been through the use of resources. After you identify the resources you need and put them to use, you'll find it easier to express your talent fully. And here's a bit of good news: *You may already have access to all the resources you need to realize your greatest hopes.*

Thomas Edison knew how critical resources were. He kept a storeroom in his West Orange, New Jersey, laboratory filled with an odd assortment of materials he collected from his well-traveled friends. The workers in his lab—each hoping to achieve some breakthrough in a particular invention—were free to check out any of these resources to see how many uses they could find for each one and how different resources worked together in creative ways.

Wouldn't it be amazing to have those kinds of resources available to you as you sought to realize your hopes? In fact, you do. They don't just exist in one room or laboratory. They are the people, places, and things all around you. And they are simply waiting for you to check them out. With search engines, social media sites, and crowdsourcing, you have a resource laboratory with millions more resources than Edison enjoyed.

Here's an approach we've used successfully to help people tap the resources they need. It focuses on how to expand your list of resources, use valuable ones more intensively, and create something new from fresh connections. Use each of the elements individually or collectively for maximum effect. We'll describe the approach first and then give you a concrete example of how it worked successfully.

Your Resource Power-Up

1. 100 Resource Challenge (list your resources and keep adding to them). Most people underestimate their resources. Now's your time to get reconnected to them. Remember, your resources can be people, places, and things. With this challenge, you gradually grow your resource treasures until you have all you need and more. Try listing all the ones you can think of and then adding one more each day for ninety days. By the time you get to one hundred (or much

sooner), you will either have achieved your objective or be well on your way.

2. 100 Percent Resource Usage Challenge (get the most from each resource). Remember when a phone was just a phone? Now you have a phone that is a memo pad, camera, game platform, computer, and more. Go through your growing list of resources and check to see if you're using everything they can provide. Target your most promising resources, and ask yourself what it would take to feel like you are getting 100 percent from that resource. By the time you feel like you are getting 100 percent from ten of your resources, you will either have achieved your objective or be well on your way.

3. Resource Mash-Up (connect available resources). A mash-up is a creative combination or mixing of content from different sources to create a new element. Whether in music, film, or software applications, mash-ups are great ways to discover new possibilities in existing resources. With this exercise, you get to connect available resources. Rather than starting from scratch, put together available components and quickly achieve results. Once a week, pick any obstacle to realizing your hope and see if a mash-up can help you to break the logjam. You can pick several resources at random and see how combining them might create something unanticipated and useful. Invite others to participate. They may see new combinations that you're missing. When you've done this successfully five or six times, you will have a powerful awareness of the possibilities around you.

Here's an example. Kim was a rising star who wanted to break through the glass ceiling of leadership in her profession. In her Talent Catalyst Conversation, Kim explored ideas about how to expand her effectiveness through compelling presentations to large audiences. She had an opportunity coming up to give a twenty-minute inspirational speech titled "Women and

Leadership: What Needs to Change?" Even though the presentation was three months away, Kim became increasingly nervous and distracted. She was to be the fourth speaker on the program following one corporate CEO and two academic researchers. She found herself doubting her ability to pull it off.

Kim decided to see if she could use her resources more effectively and make the presentation a smashing success. Here's her use of the Resource Power-Up combination.

Kim's Resource Power-Up

Step 1

100 Resource Challenge: List her resources and keep adding to them.

Personal story, PowerPoint, jokes, support team, computer, title of the program, business suit.

Each day for the next ten days she added one more resource to the list:

My notes, the lecture hall, microphone, search engine, new articles, the audience, questions, presentation coach, the other presenters, interpersonal communication skills.

Step 2

100 Percent Resource Usage Challenge: Get the most from each resource.

Support team ... Could I be asking more from them? Let's have a sixty-minute teleconference to get their ideas, feedback, and advice.

Previous speakers ... Ask the speakers ahead of me to give me advance copies of their presentations so that I can create a fitting finale [idea from the support team meeting].

Microphone ... I don't need to be the only person in the room using a mic. I could pass it through the audience. This will open up more possibilities for audience participation and make the presentation more about them and less about me.

Lecture hall … The conversation does not need to end in the room. I can set up a LinkedIn group that members of the audience can join to continue the conversation and create a powerful network.

Step 3

Resource Mash-Up: Connect available resources.

Kim put four items in the mash-up: her own story, the material from the other presenters, the question in the conference's title of "Women and Leadership: What Needs to Change?", and the audience. She came up with a number of possibilities, but here's the one she used.

Use my presentation time to (a) summarize what's come before and (b) ask the audience a new question: "How do you need to change?" Work with the audience and their responses while weaving in my own story.

With this experience, Kim's anxiety about her presentation turned into excitement. She learned a valuable lesson along the way: she had access to far more resources than she had ever imagined.

TALENT TAKEAWAY

In order to grab opportunities to grow, first you need to see them. To get there, you can choose an open frame of mind that will help you to succeed. As much as what you *do* is important, the inner qualities of *who you are* while doing these things will ultimately determine your effectiveness. With these elements in place, you can readily find and develop the resources needed to pursue attractive opportunities.

TAKE CHARGE

Tap these powerful exercises to keep you growing and your talent flowing:

> Open yourself to grow. Try the Recipe for Growth to look for opportunities to grow, question what feels fixed, and challenge yourself to keep open. Use the Inner Quality Checklist to ensure that you are embodying your best qualities in order to attract and develop desirable opportunities.
>
> Enjoy the Resource Power-Up to expand your resources, use them more effectively, and create potent combinations.

Chapter 6

CHALLENGE YOURSELF TO STRETCH

I have been impressed with the urgency of doing. Knowing is not enough; we must apply. Being willing is not enough; we must do.

LEONARDO DA VINCI

To launch yourself forward and live a rich life of talent expression, you need to be willing to stretch beyond your present comfort zone. When we say stretch, we are talking about *healthy stretches*. To get going, we'll help you to see yourself through a new lens and give you tools that will power up your talent under every circumstance — not in some ideal world but right where you are today.

With today's hectic pace, many of us already feel stretched to capacity. We've been there ourselves and have helped thousands of people to overcome these obstacles and move ahead. We've also discovered that having powerful support in place is an absolute necessity. Thus, we'll show you how to pull together your own Talent Fulfillment Team to cheer you on and catch you when you fall, making sure that you have what you need from beginning to end.

MAKE A HEALTHY STRETCH

Have you noticed how your brain comes alive when faced with just the right amount of challenge? We like to call that a healthy stretch. A stretch helps us pay attention to what we are doing. When we feel ourselves stretching, we know that we are growing.

What's the right amount of stretch for you to stay focused on fulfilling your talent and growing sustainably?

Dr. Carol Scott describes this dynamic in her book, *Optimal Stress: Living in Your Best Stress Zone*. She notes that some stress creates a dynamic tension that attracts our brain's attention. It pulls us out of autopilot and engages our faculties. She describes the concept of flow as "a state of being in which you are fully engaged and challenged and able to apply your skills in a positive, productive way."[1]

A simple metaphor that we use is how a rubber band stretches. With little or no stretch, the rubber band doesn't fulfill its task. When stretched too far, the rubber band breaks. The same holds true for us. As illustrated in figure 5, with little or no stretch, we become disengaged or cruise along on autopilot. With too much stretch, we become frazzled and overloaded. The healthy stretch lies somewhere between autopilot and frazzled. Exactly where it occurs for you may vary according to the circumstances. When you are taking on something new, you may pause to consider what's at stake, the risks, the rewards, and your personal style of dealing with challenges. What have been healthy stretches for you?

Talent-wise, where are you on the stretch continuum? At this

Figure 5. Finding a healthy stretch

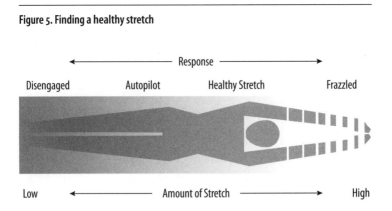

Response

| Disengaged | Autopilot | Healthy Stretch | Frazzled |

Low ← Amount of Stretch → High

moment, do you need more or less stretch to make the most of your talent?

DO YOU NEED A BIGGER STRETCH?

Sometimes we get a little too comfortable and complacent, settling into a scenario that serves us superficially but doesn't inspire or engage us. That's where Dan found himself.

Dan saw that he was on autopilot. For more than ten years, Dan had worked in production. He was one of the unsung heroes who figured out how to make the products that the hot-shot designers developed. When he thought about making a healthy stretch, he realized that he was almost totally disengaged from his work. "The pay's OK, but I feel like I'm just a cog in the wheel." Through his Talent Catalyst Conversation, he determined that he wanted his career to be invigorating rather than draining. Dan wanted more than a paycheck.

What stretch could get Dan cooking again? He thought about how to refocus on what he enjoyed about his work and making a bigger contribution to how his company developed and produced new products. He decided to challenge himself to formulate a state-of-the art document that would track how to make effective products from the sometimes less-than-useful plans that the designers developed. He figured that if he worked with his peers to detail their creative process, coworkers and supervisors would understand and possibly value their work more highly. He would gain the recognition that he missed, and the business would benefit from a clearer and more effective process.

What if Dan's innovation and initiative went unnoticed? Even if he wasn't recognized, Dan figured that it would be worth rising to the challenge and feeling better about himself along the way. As it turned out, he not only documented the process but also ended up improving it.

If you feel disengaged or stuck on autopilot, you need a

healthy stretch. As you're reading this, what ideas about healthy stretches come to mind? If, at this point in the book, you haven't yet had a Talent Catalyst Conversation, we highly recommend it. The open-ended questions will help you to see fresh ways to move toward your hopes.

It behooves you to take charge of your talent and get engaged in your career, whether or not your organization encourages it. Disengagement not only stifles your talent but also undermines your health. A Gallup study of 9,561 employed adults from February 2008 through April 2009 concluded that "actively disengaged employees were 1.7 times as likely as engaged employees to report being diagnosed with anxiety for the first time in the next year. And actively disengaged employees were almost twice as likely as engaged employees to report being diagnosed with depression for the first time in the next year."[2] You've undoubtedly seen this pattern for yourself. When people become disengaged, they find outlets elsewhere to stimulate their brains or even numb their frustration. It might be alcohol, drugs, gambling, excessive personal risk taking, or something else. In contrast, when you are putting your talent to its best use, other parts of your life benefit as well.

GOING BEYOND A STRETCH — DO YOU NEED A BIG LEAP?

You've probably seen it in the movies: a rooftop chase where our hero runs at top speed, attempting to escape the pursuit. Then suddenly there is no place to go. The only choices are to surrender or attempt to leap across an alleyway to the next rooftop. That's the way life is sometimes, metaphorically speaking. A person has stretched as far as he can go and has found himself in an uncomfortable place. He can either go back or take a big leap forward.

When Fran decided to step outside the confines of her staff role and find a path to become a supervisor, she took a big leap by inviting the CEO of her company to become part of her personal Talent Fulfillment Team. When Dan decided to document an effective process for his company, he stretched beyond the status quo and got engaged. What kind of big leap might you need to take to fulfill your hopes? Depending on your circumstances, your big leap could involve something as simple as requesting help when you need it or moving in a fresh direction at work.

ARE YOU A CANDIDATE FOR A BIG LEAP?

How can you tell if it's time to consider a big leap? There is an old story about a man on a journey who one night found himself clinging desperately to the edge of a cliff. All he could do was concentrate on holding on and not falling into the gaping chasm he imagined was below. As the sun came up, he began to see other people walking around him. Strangely, they appeared to be almost at eye level. When he summoned the courage to look down, he realized that his feet were only inches from the ground at the base of the cliff. He let go of the thing he had held on to and continued on his journey.

Funny thing about these old stories—sometimes they have lasted a long time because there is truth to them. Is there something you've held on to because of an unfounded fear that letting go would be too dangerous—for example, looking into changing departments or asking to shadow an expert in your field once a month? What's your leap? Would letting go allow you to continue on your journey?

A leap forward is worth taking even if you might fall. Chad learned this at the end of the ropes course he tried in a midcareer challenge workshop. Chad had proudly succeeded in all the other sections of the course and felt pretty confident about himself until he came to the section they called the "Heebie-Jeebies." The setup was a single thin steel cable strung sixty feet above hard-packed earth. Several other cables crisscrossed the single cable at sharp angles. He didn't see how he could get his body to the other end of the hundred-foot stretch without a hitch.

Confronted with the "Heebie-Jeebies," Chad faced a choice: "Will I go forward to finish the ropes course knowing that I will likely fall, or will I turn back?" Turning back didn't appeal to him at all. Therefore, even though he couldn't figure out in advance how he could make it all the way across, Chad decided to move forward.

Chad did step out on the steel cable … and he did fall. Had he been reckless or careless? Absolutely not. He knew that hundreds of others had done the "Heebie-Jeebies" before him and none of them had died or been injured. He also knew that he was on belay with two people on the ground who agreed to spot him and keep the tension tight on the ropes and pulleys holding his harness so that if he did fall, he might get a few bruises from the cables but wouldn't crash to the ground.

Chad's experience of a "big leap" was literal. He and his companions on this career course learned in their bones, and with a few bruises, that no matter how much success you've enjoyed, there will be times when you have to take a big leap to move forward. Just be sure you have the support you need to manage the risks.

OVERLOADED? TOOLS TO CARE FOR YOURSELF

Let's move back to the other end of the spectrum, the realm of being frazzled and overloaded. If you are at that place, you need to take immediate steps to make your situation more manageable and create the potential for solid growth.

It is not that unusual for people to reside in the frazzled-to-overwhelmed region of the stress scale, for a myriad of reasons — kids, career, health issues, financial struggles, relationship problems, family conflicts, a lawsuit, accident, or a family member being deployed overseas, to name a few.

Even if you've stretched yourself way beyond what's healthy, how can you pull back so that you rely more on your talent than on willpower? It is possible to evolve from surviving to thriving. To do so, we suggest a great focus on self-care and a reexamination of your story. Taking charge of your talent first requires taking care of yourself. Part of taking care of yourself may involve changing your story from "I have to do this all myself" to "It's time to bring in the reinforcements and have a better quality of life right here and right now."

If you're overwhelmed, there are things you can do today to ease back toward the healthy stretch zone.

1. **Reexamine your story.** What is your story? Are you doing it all alone? Has the pressure built up to an overwhelming crescendo? If so, how could you tweak your story, even slightly, to allow yourself to begin to be in balance and enjoy using your talent?

2. **Do more of what you like (and have something to look forward to).** Make a list of everything you like and even love to do, and begin adding items from that list to your daily schedule. Are there simple activities you could add to your daily life, or friends you could get together with, that would help you to feel more balanced?

3. **Create or enlist a team of support people.** Identify two or three people in your life who support you and are interested in your well-being. Can you ask them if they would be interested in being there for you in whatever way served you best? Many times, people are hesitant to ask for support at first and are relieved to find out that when they do, those around them often want to chip in.

4. **Delegate, delegate, delegate.** How could you delegate responsibilities in your own life—either at work, at home, or both? Are there members of your family who could support you on a regular basis? Do you have friends who would love to help you out?

Self-care may seem indulgent on the surface, but if you think of yourself as being like a car, you will realize just how important it is to take care of yourself so that you don't run on fumes and end up stranded and broken down. Sometimes we zoom ahead and don't notice the little warning signs along the road that guide us to slow down for just a moment and recharge. The more you take care of yourself, the better you will feel in everything you do and about everyone with whom you do it.

ENLIST YOUR TALENT FULFILLMENT TEAM

Nobody accomplishes anything important on his or her own. Even though you are the hero of your own talent story, or in the process of becoming the hero, remember that heroes have a strong supporting cast. The people around you can provide tremendous support—and the possibility of receiving that support can easily go unnoticed unless you take a moment to look through a new lens.

In the Talent Catalyst Conversation, your Catalyst asked you whom you would like to have on your personal Talent Fulfillment Team. Do you have a team in place? If you don't—and even if you do—you will benefit from the following exercise. The right team makes a critical difference between experiencing just a burst of talent and talent with staying power.

From the people you listed as resources, we will show you how to pull your Talent Fulfillment Team together just as a manager would pull together a team for a new project: with a staffing plan, job requirements, and goals to meet. Who would be the star players on your team? How do you recruit them? Here are some of the kinds of support roles we've seen people include in their plans: coworkers, mentors, subject matter experts, friends and family, coaches, advisors, cheerleaders, Hope Holders, champions, researchers, assistants, writers, referral sources, managers, and partners—to name a few.

So, what does your Talent Fulfillment Team roster look like?

Take some time to sketch out the kinds of support you need, and for each of them identify potential players, the requests you'd like to make, and the results you hope to achieve.

Now, what if you identify people for your Talent Fulfillment Team, but you worry about whether they will be willing and available? Or perhaps you just don't like asking people for help. This is understandable. Asking for help requires a certain degree of vulnerability, which isn't always comfortable. In fact, many people make up stories to protect themselves from situations like this: "I don't want to take advantage of anyone." "I ought to be able to do this myself." "I don't want to be in anyone's debt."

One great inner quality to employ when thinking about asking for support is generosity. Asking for and receiving help is a way to prime the pump of generosity. When you make a request, you are giving another person a chance to contribute to your well-being. If the person is unable or unwilling to say yes to your request, you might try asking the person what he or she would be willing to do or if he or she could recommend other people who might be interested in the role. In any event, maintain a high regard for whatever response the person gives you.

Many people choke when it comes to asking others for help. Maybe you have your own self-limiting comments, like "He's probably too busy. Why would he want to help me?" Yes, helpful, well-connected people are busy, and yes, you need to make your case for them to help you. Making *effective* requests of others is critical to helping us all learn how to work together in a way that benefits everyone.

There are four important elements to making effective requests. Let's look at how you can put intention, observation, request, and confirmation into action to secure your Talent Fulfillment Team.

> **Express your intention.** Before making your request, state clearly what you hope to accomplish and why it is of value. This lets people know what you envision. If possible, link

something of value to the person you are making the request of in order to create an everyone-wins situation.

Provide a clarifying observation. Describe what you see that sets the context for your request. Use "I" statements. For example, "I notice ..." Include just the facts, no editorial comments or judgments.

Make a request. Make a simple, direct statement of what you want, and ask whether the person is willing to provide it. Be brief and direct. Otherwise, people may feel crowded and pressured. Deliver the request and wait for the other person to respond. Give the person permission to accept, reject, or modify the request to work for both of you.

Close with a confirmation. The last step in a healthy request process is to restate and confirm whatever you have agreed upon. For instance, if the person has promised to supply you with some material by the end of the week, confirm by asking if he or she would like a reminder or a follow-up call. The purpose here is twofold: to make sure you get what you need and to keep the relationship from becoming clouded by differing expectations.

Remember Fran's interest in getting the CEO of her organization to be on her Talent Fulfillment Team? For a staff member, that's quite a reach. Here's an illustration of Fran making a bold request.

Intention: "I enjoy guiding and supporting people, and would like to become a manager and support our organization's continued success." Notice how Fran has made a link between her intention and something of value to the CEO.

Observation: "I see that supervisory positions require experience in leading teams and giving performance feedback."

Notice how the observation provides a context that links the intention with the request that follows.

Request: "I would like very much to join the Hudson River Project, if I could serve in a leadership role so that I can get more supervisory experience." Notice the simple, short request. Tom, the CEO, appreciated the clarity of Fran's request and agreed to help. The project she requested was already fully staffed, but he offered to open up thirty minutes on his schedule to discuss other possibilities coming up where Fran could lead teams and provide performance feedback.

Confirmation: "OK, I'll contact your assistant today and make a thirty-minute appointment." Notice how the confirmation makes clear who, what, and when for the action.

This process works because it is personal and direct. People will clearly know your intent and understand both the context and your request. You'll enjoy success if you have no expectations about a specific outcome. Whether or not someone accepts a particular request is entirely his or her choice. This perspective will free you to request what you really want.

Is there a request that you'd like to make of someone? Think of something meaningful that will help expand your opportunities around fulfilling your hopes. Take a few minutes to write out your request and practice it with someone before you make the request of the person you want to engage. Remember, an effective request follows the simple format of intention, observation, request, and confirmation. If you feel uncomfortable approaching this action, try practicing with smaller requests first. However, don't be afraid to reach further than you have in the past. Tapping into the abundant resources that people in your life possess and can share may reveal unexpected opportunities for realizing your hopes.

DEVELOP YOUR TALENT ACTION PLAN (TAP IT!)

Now it's time to create a game plan that will consolidate all your efforts and empower you to move forward. This is where all the dreams you've had about bringing your talent to life come solidly down to earth. Your Talent Action Plan is your own personal road map, and you are in the driver's seat for this journey.

Your Talent Catalyst Conversation gave you a starting point for moving forward. The Talent Action Plan guides you to nail down the details involved in taking action, such as accessing resources, allotting time, and gaining the support you need. It's also something you can share with your supervisor and members of your Talent Fulfillment Team so that they can quickly see where you are headed and how they can help. When you get your plan down on paper and share it with others, you will have declared your intentions and will gain an added rush of interest and energy from your own commitment.

Remember Sheila, the manager who wanted to clear some of the tasks off her very full plate? In her Talent Catalyst Conversation, she expressed a hope to work on bigger, more critical projects. She headed up a highly valued accounting group and wanted to broaden her impact but already felt swamped. She thought her team was filled to the brim as well. Thus, she was afraid to take on more or put more on anyone else. Sheila wanted to make room to pursue her aspirations, but she felt stuck. She decided to see if putting everyone's brains to work on the problem might bring fresh solutions. When she did a Talent Catalyst Conversation with each of her team members, she discovered that they also wanted to grow. Some of the responsibilities she wanted to let go of were things others wanted to learn.

Sheila definitely encountered many obstacles in her quest to work on bigger projects and to find more personal fulfillment from her work. But her Talent Action Plan helped set her and her team on the right track. It gave her a clear path that she could return to in order to keep making progress. See her responses to the TAP It! below.

Sheila's Talent Action Plan (TAP It!)

Your hopes: *Broaden my perspectives and enhance my contributions to critical issues facing our organization.*

1. What needs to be learned or developed for you to realize your hopes?

   Gain a better understanding of critical issues, concerns, and priorities for the organization and the challenges faced by departments and the impact on their operations.

2. Why does it need to be done?

   Broaden my perspectives and prepare for possible promotional opportunities within the organization.

3. How will it occur?

   Continue to participate in cross-departmental projects, seek out new projects, and participate in conferences.

4. Who needs to be involved?

   Experts from other divisions and departments.

5. When will it be completed?

   Ongoing, with one project completed within three months.

6. Projected resources (number of hours, cost, coaching support, etc.) to complete it?

   Five to ten hours per week, depending on items due.

7. Impact on other priorities?

   May need to delegate some routine tasks to others.

8. Reporting needs and coaching support to track progress and sustain results?

   Meet all due dates set by lead staff. Check in monthly with members of my Talent Fulfillment Team.

Sheila discovered that her Talent Action Plan also provided an excellent template for delegating work to her team members. Much to Sheila's delight, her team members came to her after their Talent Catalyst Conversations with an eagerness to take on new tasks and develop new skills. For this to work, however, Sheila and her staff needed to define and agree upon the tasks clearly enough that her staff knew what to do and that Sheila didn't become a "helicopter" manager—hovering over them to make sure that they did everything correctly.

Could the same questions help you to move forward and make a plan? Even if you aren't sure about the specifics, you will benefit from completing a draft so that others can help you to develop it further. If you have trouble getting started, ask someone to interview you with the TAP It! outline. As the person hears your answers, he or she can write down your responses. Within about twenty minutes, you'll have a Talent Action Plan and someone who can cheer you onward.

Your Talent Action Plan (TAP It!)

Your hopes: [brief statement of your aspirations that the Plan will address]

1. What needs to be learned or developed for you to realize your hopes?
2. Why does it need to be done?
3. How will it occur?
4. Who needs to be involved?
5. When will it be completed?
6. Projected resources (number of hours, cost, coaching support, etc.) to complete it?
7. Impact on other priorities?
8. Reporting needs and coaching support to track progress and sustain results?

Look for opportunities to brainstorm your plan with other people who have similar objectives. For example, after more than 150 managers and professional staff members in a Silicon Valley organization completed their Talent Catalyst Conversations, they gathered for a follow-up workshop to turn their intentions into action. With their draft Talent Action Plans in hand, they formed small TAP It! groups around shared topics. They organized themselves by topic, including becoming a manager, leading projects, and leaving a legacy. The room was abuzz with people comparing their Talent Action Plans—brainstorming ways to expedite their progress and encouraging one another. With this exercise to support them, as well as their teamwork and camaraderie, they spurred each other on to stretch and deliver. In the process, they also brought a bubble-up culture of talent development to life.

TAKE CONSISTENT ACTION WITH A DAILY TALENT ACTION PACK

The Daily Talent Action Pack is a creative way to break bigger projects into bite-sized actions. Using the Daily Action Pack will provide you with a form of accountability, give you helpful reminders, and help you to develop attainable ways of staying connected to your hopes. You can use the Daily Talent Action Pack with the Talent Action Plan or as a standalone exercise.

The Daily Talent Action Pack is a group of actions you take each day, at least five days a week, that when completed add up to realizing your hope. It establishes the consistent actions you need to accomplish what's truly important to you. It also gives you a way of completing your work each day with a sense of progress and pride.

You can employ the Daily Talent Action Pack in two different ways:

> **By time, number of actions, or results.** For example, thirty minutes exercising, send fifteen e-mails to support your plan, close one sale of a new service you've developed.

As an exercise of daily points earned. (Play for a number of points per day or total for the week.) For example, thirty minutes exercising (3 points), fifteen e-mails (10 points), close one sale (25 points), with a target of 30 points a day or 100 points per week.

Let's revisit Fran's story. Here is an example of what a Daily Talent Action Pack might look like for Fran. Since she likes games and quick rewards, the daily-points-earned format appealed to her.

A Daily Talent Action Pack for Fran

Target: 10 points per day

Spend twenty minutes researching performance feedback online (3 points).

Have one conversation with a coworker about his or her experiences of receiving performance feedback (4 points).

Sit in on a performance feedback session (10 points).

Interview a manager about his or her knowledge about performance feedback (10 points).

Read a chapter in a book about performance feedback (3 points).

No matter which style suits you better, feel free to adapt or change your lists to meet your needs. If you find that you consistently avoid one action item, simply take it off the list and see if you can find a better one to replace it. The Daily Talent Action Pack is a tool to assist you, not wear you down. Tweak it until it feels right, and adjust it as needed. A manager found it helpful to create Daily Talent Action Pack cards and write the points on them. It reminded him of collecting baseball trading cards.

He liked how it encouraged him not only to collect points for smaller steps, which were easy and immediately rewarding, but also to complete some tougher items worth more points.

SLICE THROUGH OVERWHELMING WORKLOADS

Many people feel overwhelmed these days, with workloads that exceed the time available. In fact, these individuals never get caught up. As a result, even thinking about what they might do to make a stretch seems like a pipe dream.

In the wake of downsizing and flatter organizations, people work more feverishly. What's more, mobile phones, pagers, and e-mail have created instant communications, and with them the expectation of instant response. No wonder so many people feel that their lives are flying out of control!

Abe, a talented manager, found himself in exactly this bind. His personal workload was about double what he was completing, and new tasks kept stacking up, which added to his frustration. Not surprisingly, Abe's hopes and plans for making better use of his talent and gaining greater satisfaction kept drifting out of reach.

The solution came when he learned about how successful surgeons managed their workloads. The first step involved prioritizing his tasks and clarifying which tasks he absolutely needed to do and which he could drop, delegate, or delay. With this approach at the ready, Abe soon became like a doctor in an emergency room and triaged his tasks. He gave primary attention to critical tasks that required immediate attention, stabilized other tasks until he could get to them, and left the remainder to wait.

The second step for Abe was to delegate projects and responsibilities to others. These included people reporting to him as well as outside resources hired on a contract basis. Fortunately, like Sheila, Abe found through Talent Catalyst Conversations with these players that they welcomed the opportunity to learn and grow—when it came from their own initiative.

Even though the first two steps reduced Abe's workload, the critical tasks that required his attention still exceeded the time available in his day. He typically started each day logging on to e-mail and responding to phone calls. Often, this absorbed his entire morning. It was late in the day before he got to the most important projects. Even then, he continued to take phone calls and respond to coworkers and people reporting to him. His schedule served everyone else's immediate needs, but it didn't serve him or his priorities.

The essential third step in getting this manager's work under control was *attention management*. Attention management applies the approach that successful surgeons use to manage their work. Surgeons identify their most productive time of day to do surgeries, usually the morning, and block it out. They complete their surgeries and then handle office visits and phone consultations later in the day. As you can imagine, it doesn't work to have office visits interrupt surgeries or surgeries interrupt office visits!

Here's how to use attention management to slice through an overwhelming workload in your business.

1. **Identify your most productive time of day.** When are you best at doing creative work or completing major projects? For most people, this is at the start of the day when they are fresh. Others may not get going until late in the day. Focus on when you are at your best, not when you have time available.

2. **Block out times for the most important projects.** Figure out how much time you need in a week to complete your high-priority tasks, especially those that will boost your talent. Schedule them in your most productive time slots.

3. **Set up a system to handle other demands during this time frame.**

Transfer your phone to voice mail. Set your e-mail so that each new one doesn't distract your attention. Put your pager in a drawer. Place a sign on your door to discourage interruptions and to let people know when you will be available.

4. **Train others to honor your schedule.** Tell your coworkers and assistants what you want to accomplish. Have them screen phone calls and other requests so that only critical demands interrupt your project time. Indicate that you will be available to answer all calls before the day is over or at defined intervals during the business day.

When Abe analyzed his schedule and the people he needed to serve and support, he realized that he didn't have to be constantly on call. He could be much more in control of his time by making himself available to others at certain times during the day and remaining committed to his own priorities during other time blocks.

5. **Sustain the practice for at least three weeks.** When you practice a new habit for three weeks or more, you dramatically increase your chances of long-term success. It takes time to shift from an adrenaline-driven pattern of immediate response to one of focused performance.

6. **Enjoy the results.**

Organizing your time and eliminating distractions can yield dramatic improvements in your results and personal satisfaction. After two weeks on his new schedule, Abe caught up with his workload and had time to spare to make rewarding progress on his Talent Action Plan. Both he and his business benefited.

Igniting your talent can begin with a single conversation; realizing the power of your talent involves engaging in action every day.

Enjoy healthy stretches and deliver on your potential!

TALENT TAKEAWAY

Forward progress and rewarding growth require healthy stretches. A Talent Action Plan, a supportive Talent Fulfillment Team, and a Daily Talent Action Pack support stepwise results. The sharp focus of a surgeon's schedule slices through even overwhelming workloads. Apply the intense focus of a surgery to pursue your hopes.

TAKE CHARGE

Determine what a healthy stretch is for you. Is it a set of small actions, or do you need a bigger leap to get where you want to be? Take a few minutes to outline your Talent Action Plan and brainstorm about it with other people. Enlist your Talent Fulfillment Team members to review your plan, and engage their support. Decide how you can translate your plan into daily progress. Identify, claim, and use your most productive times in your day or week to create space for your hopes to flourish.

Key #3

MULTIPLY THE PAYOFFS FOR YOURSELF AND OTHERS

All people want to be known and valued for their knowledge and skills. They want their talent to matter. We think of "matter" in two senses. One meaning describes making talent into something of substance, as in concrete and tangible. The other meaning relates to making a difference for ourselves and others. Both dimensions contribute to fulfillment.

Do you want to make your talent matter in ways that offer valuable returns on your investment? If so, take a page from successful Silicon Valley venture companies that create world-changing businesses and earn extraordinary returns. How do they do it? They transform knowledge and skills into tangible assets, offering products and services that people want. Once they produce these assets, they can market them to many people with limited extra effort or cost. The businesses that become powerful brands and "go viral" like Google and Apple become smashing successes.

Key #3 shows how you can apply the concepts of the venture business model to be a successful *human capital investor* in yourself and your organization. You'll gain the power to convert your talent into career assets you can brand to attract the opportunities you want. It doesn't matter whether you are an office clerk, factory worker, teacher, or manager. You don't need your talent to be "the best thing since sliced bread" to gain a big payoff. You can simply take the knowledge and skills you have developed while taking charge of your talent and get them working powerfully for you.

As you share your talent with others in ways they can use, your talent—your brand—will spread and free you up to grow even more successfully. Everyone wins. When you champion a take-charge talent culture, you help these tools to go viral for more people to enjoy.

Chapter 7

CREATE ENDURING CAREER ASSETS

Are you crazy? Stick my face on the label of salad dressing?
PAUL NEWMAN

As a rugged actor and race-car driver who played mostly tough-guy roles, Paul Newman couldn't imagine that his face would end up on salad dressing labels. But the Newman's Own food label has given more than $330 million to charities across the globe. Newman was quoted as saying, "The embarrassing thing is that the salad dressing is outgrossing my films."[1] The actor hoped to support humanitarian causes and ultimately turned his talent into an asset—and a brand—that made massive contributions to the world.

So what does this have to do with you? Believe it or not, you too can turn your talent into solid and transferable assets, and you don't have to be one of the most famous people on the planet to do it. A clear formula will guide you to create career assets using your unique talent, no matter what your specialty or position. As you build your own personal brand, you will communicate powerfully *who you are* and *what you are all about* so that others will see you shine at first glance.

A TALE OF TWO TALENTS

Let's compare two talented and dedicated people.

Sarah is a top sales rep for her financial products company.

She consistently places in the top five for her international firm. Everyone loves her energy and willingness to take on newbies and train them to be powerful players. She is unafraid that she'll lose ground if others succeed. Sarah knows that everyone has to work together to keep their company profitable in a rapidly changing field. To help communicate with her team, Sarah created a detailed template that clearly captures the steps of her effective sales-pitch process. She constantly updates and improves her template and keeps her team on top of everything she does so that they can reap the rewards together.

Then there is Matt. Matt manages the project calendar for his firm's software product releases. He is the go-to guy to make sure that his firm meets clients' needs on time, every time. His team members get automated reminders of task due dates, and as a result, they rarely miss a beat. Although Matt could be known as the killer project manager, he is not because no one realizes all the work that has gone into his successful approach. If Matt weren't there to run the project timeline programs, everything would fall apart.

Matt and Sarah, both highly talented people, have a gap between them—Sarah figured out how to turn her talent into assets and Matt did not.

Talent has its fullest meaning when it is translated into results that are both concrete and replicable. No one wants their hard efforts to evaporate and be irrelevant to others. If Matt decided to change jobs, his legacy might not follow him because it's not documented or usable by others. Also, there would be no way for his boss to see the value of all his work. His expertise might be overlooked when it came time to provide references. If Matt's job were suddenly eliminated, his entire department could fall apart. No one else knows how to access the creative and accurate programs he developed. On the other hand, Sarah was able to take what she was best at and package it in a way that others could understand and use so that everyone could fly.

SEE ONE, DO ONE, TEACH ONE: MAKE YOUR TALENT TANGIBLE

You may clearly see the value of creating assets from your talent, but where to begin? Let's check out how Fran used her Talent Catalyst Conversation and Talent Action Plan to create assets that later enabled her to become a manager, which was her long-term hope. Here are the steps she took:

> Fran's Talent Catalyst Conversation inspired her to figure out commonsense ways that she could use the requirements for her master's degree program and on-the-job experience to become skilled in giving performance feedback.
>
> She used her Talent Action Plan to create a plan of action.
>
> She wrote a research paper on best practices for one of her courses.
>
> She learned from experts by shadowing her HR director and others as they gave performance feedback.
>
> She enlisted a trusted manager to do a mock performance feedback session with her, and the manager played the role of a tough employee.
>
> Finally, Fran gained approval to give constructive performance feedback to three team members on their special project.

Still, how would her book learning and feedback to project team members stack up against the line management experience of an outside candidate? Despite all her efforts, Fran knew that she needed to make her knowledge and skills more tangible—showing something more concrete and delivering greater résumé value. Instead of giving up, Fran relied on an old surgeons' method called "See one, do one, teach one."

When a surgeon wants to learn a new procedure, he or she scrubs up with a surgeon experienced in the procedure and observes it firsthand. Then, the learner does the next surgery with a surgeon experienced in the procedure overseeing it. Finally, the surgeon newly trained on the procedure teaches the procedure to another surgeon. As everyone who teaches knows, when you teach someone else, you learn very deeply. In other words:

1. You observe an expert.
2. You practice with an expert guiding you.
3. When you are ready, you teach what you have learned to others.

Fran was ready to teach others how to give performance feedback. For this, she needed tangible tools. So she created a draft checklist of best practices. She shared it with expert managers, who gave her feedback and comments, which helped her greatly to refine her checklist and bring it to life. Finally, Fran developed a brief guide on performance feedback for first-time supervisors. The product, and the drive and smarts she used to pull it together, impressed her bosses.

Figure 6 shows how Fran translated her new knowledge and skills into assets and opportunities.

Figure 6. Fran's "see one, do one, teach one."

See One:	Fran learned how to provide good performance feedback by observing experts and learning how they did it.
Do One:	Under the guidance of experts, Fran demonstrated her performance feedback skills in mock and real-life project settings.
Teach One:	Fran showed others with a set of written guidelines how to tackle one of the toughest challenges of managing—giving candid, constructive performance feedback, especially to friends and peers.

YOUR TURN

How do *you* translate *your* talent into career assets? First, think about what you want to accomplish. Then, describe your knowledge, skills, or abilities in the context of what you want to create to move forward. Use figure 7 to stimulate your thinking about ways to convert your knowledge and skills into solid career assets. If you are feeling stumped, ask a friend or a coworker to be a generous listener for you. Choose someone who knows something about you and what your opportunities are like. Ideally, that person can help you to translate your knowledge and skills into a career asset vocabulary that will give you clarity.

Plug your hopes into the "See one, do one, teach one" formula to put your assets into action.

> **See one:** Team up with an expert in your field and watch the person in action—observe closely as he or she does the very thing you dream of doing yourself.

> **Do one:** Ask that expert, or some other qualified person, to oversee you as you "take your first cut" and try out your new abilities for yourself. Make sure to ask for feedback and constructive criticism so that you can shorten your learning curve.

Figure 7. Tangible talent.

Knowledge and Skills	Career Assets
What are you on the verge of creating with your talent, skills, knowledge, insights, or abilities?	How does this creation translate into something of value to others?
What is your goal — in what direction do you want to move?	How will your progress contribute to the organization or to your field?
What are you learning, or what do you already know in this area, that will facilitate the process?	How can you make this learning or knowledge concrete and tangible for others to appreciate and use?

Teach one: Document what you've learned, and teach it to others to show that you've mastered the skill and have a valuable career asset.

BUILD A POWERFUL PERSONAL BRAND

Fran had two distinctive personal advantages that served her career beautifully. First, she had the drive to learn in order to pursue her deepest hopes. Second, she lived with one of the biggest challenges in giving performance feedback—giving feedback to peers and friends (since she was not yet a supervisor).

All this translated into a powerful personal brand for Fran. Others saw her as someone who both cared deeply about the people she worked with and provided candid, constructive performance feedback. Instead of being viewed as someone who had gone to the dark side of managerial power plays, she illuminated how to accomplish results and still enjoy the respect and support of people she led.

Branding pioneer Walter Landor said, "A brand is a promise that creates a preference."[2] What about *your* brand—what do you want to promise so that people or organizations have a preference for you? A clear personal brand communicates what you have to offer and attracts desirable opportunities. When you combine your brand—plus proof of your brand delivering value for others, you create opportunities for yourself.

As figure 8 illustrates, it's a simple but powerful formula.

We see in figure 9 how this formula worked for Fran as she positioned herself.

Now that we see how Fran successfully branded herself, let's look at Tony, a police chief. Tony felt stuck and wanted to explore broader career opportunities in local government. "My problem is that everyone just sees me as a police chief. I feel pigeonholed." Cities with general management openings didn't see how the chief's skills would transfer. He needed some tangible career assets and a fresh brand.

Tony reached out to a colleague outside of his organization to help him get a fresh perspective on his situation. Here are some snippets from their discussion.

COLLEAGUE: What's interesting to you in your job at this time, and what are you learning about it?

TONY: I'm leading a major project to establish collaboration among police departments in the region to share services, improve response, and reduce costs.

COLLEAGUE: Wow, the skills to accomplish that sound like the talents that many general management jobs require. How could you translate those into assets that would grab the interest of organizations looking for general managers?

TONY: I could write up what I am doing as a case study for publication in a journal read by city managers and elected

---

Figure 8. Build your brand formula.

Brand	+	Proof Points	=	Opportunities for You
Your promise that creates a preference for your talents/services		Career assets or what you "have to offer"		What you want to be doing

---

Figure 9. Fran's brand formula.

Brand	+	Proof Points	=	Opportunities for You
"I want to be known for my ability to bring out the best in others through candid, constructive feedback, even in the difficult situations when people are friends or former peers." Brand: *Candid, constructive feedback that brings out the best in you*		Demonstrated skills to key managers and team members Checklist guide of best practices for giving performance feedback for first-time supervisors		• Qualification for a supervisory position • Particularly attractive candidate for results-oriented roles requiring collaboration

officials. In fact, one of the editors had mentioned that he was interested in my project, but I didn't think too seriously about it until now.

Tony began the process of rebranding himself from "police chief managing law enforcement" to "leader guiding innovation in tough budget times."

How do you establish your brand, compile your proof points, and create a compelling case for the opportunities you seek? You can use the same formula as Fran did above: identify your brand, collect your proof points, and take a close look at the possibilities that your *branding* could create. The formula works in both directions. You can start with your brand, identify proof points, and then see what opportunities open up for you. Or, as Tony did, you can start with the opportunities you'd like to pursue and then figure out the proof points and brand message that you'd need to attract them.

Like a radio station, you need to broadcast a strong signal to attract the audience and opportunities you seek. What's more, an effective brand will have people telling your story to others. You can be creative and find ways to build your career assets in any situation. Current circumstances and positioning needn't keep you from developing and pursuing your talents to fulfill your hopes.

This is a valuable topic, and you can have a lot of fun with it. If you are taking a first-time look at creating your own personal brand, you may want substantial support. Getting together with someone who knows you well and understands both your assets and your hopes will help you to brainstorm ideas.

TALENT TAKEAWAY

When it comes to your talent, translate the intangible into the tangible. As you create assets, you bring your talent into the realm of what's solid and demonstrable. Your personal brand is "a promise that creates a preference," and the proof points are your tools to attract what you want.

TAKE CHARGE

Pick a talent (knowledge, skill, or ability) that you'd like to develop. Use the surgeon's method of "See one, do one, teach one" to learn it. Make the results into something tangible (a checklist, how-to video, etc.) that becomes a career asset for you. Define your brand, and use the career assets as proof points to open up opportunities to fulfill your hopes.

Chapter 8

SHARE THE WEALTH AND EVERYONE WINS

We want an organization of 20,000 learners and 20,000 teachers.

JUDY GILBERT, DIRECTOR OF TALENT, GOOGLE

Sharing our talent makes for a better world. Can you imagine living without good books, great movies, delicious food, techie devices, and the music you listen to on your way to work? Someone's talent lies behind every expression of creativity that you value in your life, from homemade peanut butter to Facebook. When you make your talent tangible, it becomes transferable. In a world full of people embodying their talents, everyone wins. In today's environment, your favorite music or performers may live thousands of miles away, but their abilities still enrich you. Likewise, small groups of scientists in Switzerland have breakthroughs that affect people in the United States, China, and Madagascar.

Tangible talent affects us on every level—personally, in our workplaces, and even at home. As you put your talent into action and make tangible career assets, and then share them with others so that they become organizational assets, you not only gain recognition but also open more room to grow for yourself and others. In turn, this expands opportunities to develop your talent. Think of it as a Talent Wheel (see figure 10). The more you contribute, the more you and your organization benefit. This regenerative process creates a culture of talent development in

Figure 10. The Talent Wheel.

which everyone thrives. Let's see how you can get your Talent Wheel spinning.

While the content of what you deliver for your organization is important, the most important thing is to get rolling in your efforts to share what you know. Maybe you've found a great way to fix a computer software problem, an effective set of steps to launch a new product, or simply a timesaving method to cut through repetitive tasks. As you value and share what you know and learn, more opportunities will arise for you.

SHARE YOUR ASSETS TO GROW FASTER

Unlike single-use commodities such as oil or gold, knowledge can be shared without incurring a cost or a loss to ourselves. In packaging your talent so that it is accessible, you increase your own savings account of career assets while helping your organization, community, or world. The more you give, the more you get back.

We've all seen the Talent Wheel turning. Why, then, does it sometimes grind to a halt? Here are some frequent issues:

I have too much on my plate to get into the nitty-gritty of teaching my coworkers how to do what I do. It's easier just to do it myself.

If I share with others what I do best, it might make me expendable.

If I teach others how to do what I do, they may gain an advantage over me and get promoted instead of me.

Whether it's expertise or ego that gets in the way of transferring knowledge, we need a better path. People hoard their talent when they aren't growing. However, when they demonstrate their expertise, pursue new opportunities, and work to leave a legacy, they will share what they know to keep growing. In short, the motivation to learn and advance becomes the impetus for us to convert personal knowledge assets into organizational assets.

If you think about it, knowledge can be either an asset or baggage that holds you down. Frequently, employees turn to those who already know something rather than learn it themselves. While this can be flattering, it's also a burden. You can't give attention to new things that you'd like to learn because you're too busy doling out rudimentary guidance. When you make a move to make your talent tangible, though, you free yourself to pursue your real interests. (See figure 11.)

Let's see how this plays out with a real-life example. In her

Figure 11. Creating organizational assets.

Personal Assets	Organizational Assets
Individual knowledge or ability that goes with the person who holds it	Shared knowledge or procedures that others can use
Comes and goes	Documented so that others can use and update it

Talent Catalyst Conversation, Sheila discovered that she needed to let go of some of her tasks—even if she was good at them—in order to grow and take on new responsibilities. Simply shifting the work around to other people, however, wasn't going to free up enough time for her to fulfill her plans.

Sheila noted that she spent a significant amount of time answering technical questions about a complex software program that many departments used. She had become the expert. The common refrain was, "Sheila, we don't know what we'd do without you."

Together, Sheila and her team found an excellent option. They wrote up procedures for handling typical situations and posted them on the organization's newly created internal wiki. Employees throughout the organization no longer needed to ask Sheila for her personal expertise. On the one hand, you could say that Sheila didn't get the praise for helping people with routine questions. However, Sheila and her team had better things to do and didn't feel the loss of indispensability on tasks they wanted to leave behind.

In this case, everyone really did win. The new procedure not only liberated Sheila and her team to move ahead but also had a profound ripple effect as their problem solving and group effort began to alter the organizational culture. When other departments witnessed how engaged and effective Sheila's team had become, they took on the same fresh approach, to the betterment of the larger organization.

TO DO OR TO STOP DOING, THAT IS THE QUESTION

Everyone knows that time is the most precious resource people have to pursue hopes for use of their talent. Yet, few of us honor it with focused attention.

Jim Collins, author of *Good to Great*, recommends a short "to do" list of no more than three essential items, and a similar "stop doing" list.[1] Just as your to-do list gets you focused on what you want to achieve, your stop-doing list helps you to clear out the clutter and make room for your desired efforts.

Do you have a few sacred cows on your to-do list—things you've done in the past that may not serve you anymore? If you punch up your to-do list with items that get you going and motivated, you'll knock off a few sacred cows more easily. If you aren't saying no to things that you have been doing, you probably aren't growing—at least not quickly.

Through your Talent Catalyst Conversation and Talent Action Plan, you've already identified what you want to be doing. Thus, you have your to-do list. So, what can you shift over to your stop-doing list? We think of it in three dimensions:

> **What can you drop altogether?** Sheila's decision to stop responding to repetitive technical questions and post the answers on the internal wiki is an example.

> **What can you delegate?** What can you offer to others for their growth and learning? That's where Sheila's team members picked up opportunities to pursue their hopes and at once freed her up.

> **What can you delay?** If you can't drop or delegate something, can you shift your priorities or schedule to make room for what you want? We used delay as part of our strategy to get the time to write this book. Interestingly, some of the urgent items we delayed faded away by the time we returned to them. For other items, when we clearly explained the delay to valuable support people, we often got help.

When you make your knowledge and skills tangible and transferable, you essentially "bottle" and share your talent so that others not only benefit from it but also can replicate the results that your talent inspired. In turn, you become free to pursue other hopes, and your own talents can further bubble up. With this generative spirit of giving, the Talent Wheel turns—for you as well as your organization.

WHAT WOULD GOOGLE DO?

Google lives up to its motto of encouraging everyone to be both a learner and a teacher. From its open system for employees to create content to its famed "testing on the toilet" (posting information in the bathroom stalls), it invites all to share what they know and doesn't miss an opportunity. Google doesn't control what employees contribute. Since users rate the content for value, the system is self-correcting.

Imagine what it would be like if Google imposed top-down control on content. How do you think a top-down approach would change the interest and eagerness with which Googlers create and contribute information? Instead of disrupting the flow, Google treats its employees as responsible adults. It focuses on *what* employees produce rather than driving *how* they do it.

Of course, Google also created a means for letting talent flow 24/7 for people around the world. The search engine and knowledge tools that it and other providers offer keep the Talent Wheel turning. As people make information from their growth available, they manifest assets and benefit organizations across the globe in a natural and symbiotic way. The good news is that you are also a part of this Talent Wheel. As you grow, you acquire knowledge and skills that you can convert into tangible career assets. When you deposit these as organizational assets, you retain the credit and create space for expansion.

Hopefully, you are in an organization or community that values your growth, encourages you to develop your career assets, and acknowledges you for sharing your contributions. But what if that's not the case?

Sometimes it's tough to gain recognition in your own milieu. As the Bible says, "No prophet is acceptable in his hometown."[2] People may have a preset or limiting view of you. Fortunately, if you are ready to share what you know, the Internet gives you an open audience. You can write a blog, post a video on a how-to site, or come up with dozens of other ways to get yourself out there. Yes, you will be "giving your expertise away," but you can gain recognition as the source. In an information-rich world, viewers will appreciate your wisdom and insight.

You may be thinking, "I don't think I have any special knowledge to offer." If you perceive your skills as being common, remember that it is not only what you know but also how you present it. A simple example is the three-minute TED talk about how to tie your shoes. Terry Moore learned that there is a strong and a weak form of tying a traditional shoelace knot. Many people unwittingly use the weak form, and their laces come undone. His video posted in May 2011 had over 1.2 million viewings by June 1, 2012.[3] Why? He shared what he learned (actually from someone else) in an engaging presentation that made his talk a sensation. This boosted his career assets as an insightful speaker and drew attention to his organization, the Radius Foundation, a forum for exploring and gaining insight from different worldviews.

Don't underestimate what you know and the value of presenting it effectively to others. Now that you've got the idea, explore how you can get the Talent Wheel turning more rapidly in your life. If you're stumped, take a page from the Googlers' playbook. Get creative. Write up your ideas and share them with friends or put them in a blog (your own or, as appropriate, someone else's). Maybe create a short video clip. Invite people to make comments and give you feedback on how to make it better. Before you know it, voilà!—you will have shared a career asset.

INVEST IN SUCCESSFUL HUMAN CAPITAL: YOUR "RETURN ON TOTAL TALENT"

You can make the payoff big from taking charge of your talent. If you share with others what you learn, you'll multiply the return on your investment. When seven to ten people acquire what you've learned, you will be earning human capital returns that parallel the seven to ten times return that venture capitalists seek.

When your career assets go viral and serve the needs of thousands and millions of people in your organization and beyond, your talent will be a runaway success. Yes, you won't be keeping all the value to yourself, but you will be raising the market value of your talent—not only what you know but, more important, what you can do with your knowledge and skills.

Does your organization recognize the value of your talent and encourage you to share your career assets so that they become organizational assets as well? Organizations that see the big picture realize that a critical measure of human capital is what employees and the organization gain from the full potential that employees have to offer. We call this measure the Return on Total Talent. It captures much more than simply what the organization spends on development of its employees and what it gets in return (return on investment). Rather, it encourages everyone to look at what he or she has to offer and how to create a much bigger pie of assets and benefits that you can enjoy together.

TALENT TAKEAWAY

Enjoy being both a learner and a teacher. When you share your career assets with your organization or community, you enhance your asset value as a source of wisdom and a valued contributor. A bubble-up culture of talent development enlists the self-motivation of employees to document and share knowledge and keeps the Talent Wheel turning for everyone.

TAKE CHARGE

Look for opportunities to share what you know with others. Deposit your proven career assets with your organization or community. Use available vehicles (internal wikis, intranets, web postings, etc.) to store, connect, and share your knowledge assets and to gain recognition for your value. See how much you can boost your Return on Total Talent.

Chapter 9

CHAMPION A TAKE-CHARGE TALENT CULTURE

We are the makers of our own fate. The wind is blowing; those vessels whose sails are unfurled catch it and go forward on their way, but those which have their sails furled do not catch the wind. Is that the fault of the wind?

NARENDRANATH DATTA

You have already come so far. What have you discovered about yourself since you opened this book? Maybe you've unearthed interests and opportunities that you never imagined. Or maybe you have begun to look at life differently. Maybe you find yourself *really* listening to your friends and coworkers when they talk about their talent. You may also find yourself more effectively pursuing your own talent. Whether you are a freelancer, an administrative assistant, or a CEO, chances are that you see possibilities and potential in yourself and others all around you—potential that you may not have noticed before.

You'll recall that in the introduction to the book, we invited you to consider how each of the items on the following checklist could benefit you, your coworkers, your organization, your family, and the rest of your life. We wanted the checklist to motivate you to see the world through a fresh and hopeful perspective. If you took us up on the invitation, it most likely started the process of bringing your hopes into reality. We thought you might enjoy looking back to see where you have made progress and how your use of the book has made a difference for you.

Your Take Charge Checklist Revisited

When you've read the book and engaged in the exercises, consider how each of the items on the following checklist has benefited you, your coworkers, your organization, your family, and the rest of your life. It is the same checklist we introduced at the beginning of the book. At that time, we asked you which of these you wanted—for example, "I want to ... make better use of my talent." Now we are asking you to see how far you've come. Check those statements where you've experienced progress. Underline those where you'd like to gain more value. You might even check and underline the same item. You always have more opportunities to grow.

I now ...

Make better use of my talent

Gain more satisfaction from my talent

Move forward in my career with gusto

Know how to turn obstacles into stepping-stones

Identify and tap the resources I need to thrive

Develop the inner qualities I need to experience
deep fulfillment

Enjoy a better balance at work where I'm neither bored
nor overloaded

Build tangible talent assets that enhance my career
and opportunities

Make a bigger contribution to others and receive recognition for it

Take pride in my work environment where everyone has
opportunities to grow

If you are now more able to take charge of your talent, that's great. Wouldn't you like others to enjoy the benefits as well and have your own efforts supported in the process? Let's explore how you can champion that potential.

BE THE CHANGE YOU WANT

Remember that everything begins with one person—an idea, an invention, a creative thought. Over time, ideas draw people together to form groups, clusters, think tanks, and even governments. Ideas are at the root of *everything*—from folk songs and languages to Fortune 500 companies. Ideas in action form businesses and organizations, and ideas in action also can *transform* them. Whether you realize it or not, every day you are living by an idea, and you are taking actions to support that idea. Living in the realm of possibility, in a culture of stretching and learning, is a new way of *being* based on a timeless idea—*we are all talented beyond our own knowing*.

Talent thrives when we choose to override our fears and invest our energy into creating an environment where everyone is free to expand. By living in the realm of possibility, stretching, and making changes in your own life, you are contributing to the creation of a self-organizing revolution that is peer driven and talent supported—a movement to revitalize the world around you by unlocking your talent.

Your example will become a powerful magnet to attract others to these practices. They'll see your positive spirit, observe you taking action, and note your efforts to share your career assets in ways that benefit you and others. Whether it's on a large or small scale, you will be championing through your deeds a take-charge culture of talent development.

As you've sparked your own talent and helped others to catalyze theirs, you may have begun to experience living in a world of talent—a world of possibility. The beauty is that everyone has talent, and we can express our talents in millions of complementary ways. As your talent shines brightly, another person's talent need not be diminished. In fact, the opposite is true. Each time you dig deeper to let more of your talent flow, you create well-being in the world. It doesn't matter if you are an artist and work by yourself in a studio all day or you are part of a multinational corporation. You, by virtue of being a human on planet Earth, are a team player. What you do, the choices you make, and the ways in which you express your unique attributes in the world make a difference—a *big* difference.

So, what's next? How can you sustain your momentum and be part of a broader effort to liberate the talents that other people yearn to articulate? Let's talk about keeping up your energy—even long after you have read this book, enjoyed a Talent Catalyst Conversation, or put your intentions into action.

STAY CHARGED UP FOR LONG-TERM RESULTS

Obstacles *will* arise as you pursue your hopes. Obstacles are like moguls on a ski slope. You can tighten up and stop, or you can see the impediments as elements that will help define your journey and increase your flexibility and enjoyment as you successfully navigate them.

Maybe you've already hit a few bumps. Perhaps you're very clear about your hopes and actions after having had a Talent Catalyst Conversation. You may even have prepared a Talent Action Plan and gained some results, but now you find yourself stalled. Did urgent needs demand your attention, leaving you without enough time to pursue new goals? Or maybe you've reached out to people you admire to be part of your Talent Fulfillment Team, only to be disappointed when they weren't available. You may even feel a little slighted. Perhaps you feel that there aren't sufficient opportunities in your organization, or you worry that the environment isn't right and your boss won't support your growth.

Have any of these concerns become the story that explains why you haven't fulfilled your aspirations? The practices in Key #2—keep your hopes humming, grab opportunities to grow, and challenge yourself to stretch—are there for you to tap whenever you need them. They offer constructive ways to shift from the fear-based stories that can get in your way to take-charge stories that keep you thriving.

In talent management, self-management plays a central role. The choices are yours. You can take charge.

ENGAGE OTHERS TO BE THEIR BETTER SELVES

As you become the change you want and stay charged up, you will attract others. Your growth, your development of tangible career assets, and your ability to share them together create the building blocks for a take-charge talent culture.

You may find that some people resist these changes. Your success may feel threatening to their stories about how they are stuck and can't act. This is understandable. We all feel some resistance when we see something that puts our stories—our view of things—into question.

One of the important principles we've learned that can help people to be their better selves and respond positively to change is to avoid making them wrong. Instead of pointing out errors or shortcomings in their approach (or the superiority of what you are doing), invite them to consider another perspective. For example, if people bemoan their work situations, ask them if they would like to share their hopes about how they want things to be. Simple questions like those you learned in the Talent Catalyst Conversation and generous listening will create openings for their better, more creative selves to come forth. Subtle efforts stimulate less resistance. As we have done with you, invite others to try the keys and observe the results for themselves. You don't need to sell them.

PROPAGATE MORE TALENT CATALYSTS

Do you want others to experience the benefits of a Talent Catalyst Conversation? Well, there are two approaches. With the direct approach, you can offer to be a Talent Catalyst for them. You've seen one with your own Conversation. When you serve as a Talent Catalyst for someone else, you add to your experience. As those of us who teach know, teaching healthy practices reinforces our own use of them. Thus, regardless of the outcome for the participants, you will benefit from offering Conversations to them.

What if people who want to use and enjoy their talents more don't step forward for a Conversation? If they haven't read about or seen a Talent Catalyst Conversation, they may be reluctant to be a participant. Do you remember all the points of concern and potential resistance discussed in chapter 1? Maybe it will help others to see the potential for themselves if you turn the tables. You could ask them to be a Talent Catalyst for you: "Look, let me show you how this works. You can be a Talent Catalyst for me and see a Conversation in action. After experiencing this, you can decide whether you'd like to have a Conversation for yourself." Once people understand how Talent Catalysts serve in supportive and nonthreatening ways, they eagerly seek to become participants themselves. Plus, you'll get some additional insights for yourself from a fresh Conversation.

SHARE THE HOPE AND GROW THE MOVEMENT

Take Charge of Your Talent arises from a core hope:

> *All people have the keys to take charge of their talent, and they enjoy using those keys to benefit themselves and others.*

We invite you to make this hope your own and to share it with others. Maybe you know people who are struggling in their careers. Perhaps you see coworkers, colleagues, or friends who have much more to contribute. Reach out to them.

WHY YOU COUNT AND WHY BEING COUNTED MATTERS

While *Take Charge of Your Talent* focuses on putting talent development into each person's hands, it is so much easier to express your talent fully when you work, play, and live in a supportive culture. "Stop banging on the piano, Wolfie!" probably wasn't something heard often in the Mozart household.

A *culture* consists of the beliefs, behaviors, objectives, and other characteristics shared by members of a cohesive and productive group. So, how would you go about encouraging a take-charge talent culture? The *Take Charge of Your Talent* Manifesto, which follows this chapter, summarizes important insights from the book. You can think of it as a set of powerful message points from which you can champion a take-charge talent culture in your work, home, and community.

As you share ideas and encourage each other, you strengthen your resolve. Those around you notice the energy and results and want to join. Thus, a community of talent development begins to emerge.

Imagine this: You share the keys with five people; they each share the keys with five more people; and the chain continues five times. In a short time, you have changed the lives of over three thousand people. When thousands of people similarly take the initiative, literally millions will start living in a world where their talent thrives more fully. Small beginnings make a huge difference. You truly do count, and that's the power of sharing what is working in your life. For additional tools to help you and your organization expand and strengthen your efforts, see "Services to Support You" in the "Resources" section.

How big can this get? Clearly, there is a large wave of need and interest. With an estimated 95 million employees not engaged in their work in the United States alone,[1] 200 million people unemployed across the globe,[2] and many others wondering if there is anything more for them in their careers, huge numbers of people and organizations need to shift gears and tap self-motivation to put more talent into action.

But how many people will step forward and embrace the opportunity? History demonstrates that people want to take charge of what's important to them. Look at the growth in the number of people buying and selling stocks on their own. In decades past, people had to rely on a personal broker to execute transactions. With the advent of online brokerage, people surged into online trading. Now, there are more than thirty million online brokerage accounts in the United States alone.[3] Wise online investors don't do it all alone. They tap information sources and talk with knowledgeable people before taking action. However, they have chosen to take charge of their financial assets themselves. Do you see the parallels with people and their talent assets—the true source of their wealth and fulfillment? Taking charge of your talent isn't going it alone, but it is taking responsibility and acting.

With our desire to empower you to go the distance in managing your own talent and the hope of sharing the keys broadly with all people, we've developed a vision. We call it the "Take-Charge 20/20 Vision":

> *By 2020, twenty million people across twenty countries will have the keys to take charge of their talent, with at least 20 percent of these people being from traditionally underserved populations—like prisons, inner-city schools, and developing countries.*

We invite you to read "Visit the Online Community" in the "Resources" section for more information and to find out how you can join the online Take-Charge Community.

You matter. Your talent matters. And together we can create a world of talent development that works for all.

FINAL THOUGHTS FOR THE JOURNEY AHEAD

This book is a story about hope. As the people in this book have demonstrated, hope is not some abstract, softheaded concept. Instead, it can be a practical and powerful way to tap the passion, energy, and creativity that lie within us. As we find hope within ourselves and translate our inspirations into opportunities through honest and open-minded conversations, we revolutionize our whole way of living—for ourselves, our organizations, and everyone who knows us. As we chart our course on the thoroughfare of flowing talent, everyone can participate. Everyone has something inimitable to contribute, and the keys and tools you've learned will keep your talent moving. Now that you have walked the walk and gained new insights and perspectives, we invite you to become an active participant in the take-charge talent movement. Everyone can join, and the best place to start is by *sharing with others how you have changed your story ... for good.*

TALENT TAKEAWAY

Each of us has important opportunities to *be* (or embody) the results we want. This will attract others to use and enjoy the keys to unlock their own talent. Anticipate bumps along the way; don't let them discourage you. And remember, you can always return to practices that will keep you charged up.

TAKE CHARGE

Follow easy steps like offering yourself as a Talent Catalyst for others so that they experience the profound power of carefully designed questions and generous listening to unlock their potential. Use the *Take Charge of Your Talent* Manifesto as a foundation to share the hope of talent development that works for all. As more people use the keys, each of you will have more support for your own growth—and we will all benefit.

THE TAKE CHARGE OF YOUR TALENT MANIFESTO

1. **We each have untapped talents and opportunities for greater satisfaction.** Satisfaction corresponds closely with how much of our talent we put to use. Experience shows that even hardworking people who are the best and brightest people in their field typically have 30–40 percent of their talent untapped. We have a wealth of opportunities to contribute to the world and improve our personal well-being. We just need help to figure out how.

2. **Accessing our hopes helps us to get out of our own way and stimulates better results.** Our brains work both to protect us and to help us grow. When we are in a hopeful frame of mind, we engage the parts of our brains that specialize in creativity, insight, and development of alternatives. We need all these faculties to tap our talents and enjoy them more fully.

3. **We can be Talent Catalysts for one another to generate new ideas and precipitate action.** With carefully targeted questions, generous listening, and a focus on action, Talent Catalyst Conversations help us to look at our careers and lives from a new angle. We can readily learn and share these conversation skills with others.

4. **Abundant resources are available to help us realize our deepest hopes.** Each of us has access to far more resources than we may think. Indeed, a useful talent is learning how to identify and attract the resources we need.

5. **We can get the time we need to pursue our hopes and take charge of our talent.** One of the biggest blocks people cite as getting in the way of their talent development is a lack of time and focus needed to pursue their hopes: "I could do it if only I had time." We can be like surgeons and slice through overwhelming workloads to do what's most valuable.

6. **The self-organizing culture of talent development creates enduring assets and fulfillment for individuals and organizations.** Pumping up the troops with inspiration from the top brass or from outsiders can feel good but is often short-lived. While inspiring leaders can give us a jump-start, we need to be running off our own batteries to stay engaged. Truly sustainable motivation rests within each of us. Trusting people to engage their hopes and giving them permission to pursue what's important to them produces results in many ways. We feel more responsible for our organizations because they become ours, as we helped to create and foster the talent that fuels them.

7. **Everyone can participate because the "See one, do one, teach one" approach supports a culture of accessible and self-organizing talent development.** Talent wants to flow freely. Indeed, the movement to take charge of your talent can go viral in the positive sense that it is a highly constructive and contagious process. As one participant learns the process, serves as a Talent Catalyst, and then teaches someone else, that person can serve and teach others. The process builds a network of learners and teachers such that talent emerges within us and all around us.

RESOURCES

FREQUENTLY ASKED QUESTIONS ABOUT THE TALENT CATALYST CONVERSATION

The Talent Catalyst Conversation Guide, in chapter 2, provides the core information you need to conduct a Conversation—narrative, questions, and cues for the Catalyst. The following frequently asked questions and answers provide opportunities for both the Talent Catalyst and the participant to delve more deeply into the dynamics of the steps and ways to navigate issues that may arise.

Round I: Enliven Your Hopes

Step 1: Connect with Your Hopes

What if the participant isn't clear about her or his hopes?

Some people may not be clear about their hopes. After all, it's not every day that people are asked about them! However, that's the freshness and value of the question. So, take some time together to explore and listen. If the Talent Catalyst doesn't see real energy or enthusiasm arising in response to the question, inquire further about what is important to the participant.

Some people fear expressing their hopes because they don't know whether other people would support them and whether their hopes are achievable. In short, fears block them. That's why

we ask participants only to express why their hopes are important to them. We don't ask them to explain their choices or
defend whether or how they might accomplish them. The steps
in Rounds II and III will help them to find pathways.

Couldn't participants simply write down their hopes on their own?

While participants could write down hopes on their own, experience shows that the presence of an attentive Talent Catalyst truly
activates deeper, more powerful insights. If participants keep
cycling on their current perspectives, they'll get into deeper ruts
rather than broader thinking and fresh perspectives.

Step 2: Consider Your Concerns

Why is this step about concerns in the "Enliven Your Hopes" round?

People typically see concerns as obstacles to realizing their
hopes. In a Talent Catalyst Conversation, however, concerns actually become another tool to help participants tap their talents.
Just as Sherlock Holmes, when confronted with a seemingly
unsolvable mystery, might say, "The game's afoot," we might say,
"Aha! A concern … what a great opportunity! I get to use my
talent to deal with this one."

*How can repeating or paraphrasing the gist of what the participant
says be of value?*

Often, people can't see or sort through all the issues and obstacles by themselves. When the Talent Catalyst reflects back what
he or she is hearing, it helps the participant to see himself or
herself more clearly. In addition, sometimes people need to talk
to figure out what they think. Everything in their mind is such
a jumble of facts, fears, and frustrations that they can't see the
forest for the trees.

Most people have the capacity to solve problems when they
have a clear understanding of the issue. If they feel stymied or
something has festered for a long time, it's likely that there's

some other issue or concern that needs attention first. That's what generous listening will help to uncover.

What if the participant's concern seems unfounded or could easily be resolved?

The Talent Catalyst must avoid the temptation to jump in and begin to either cajole or console the person. You can't be an effective catalyst if you become consumed in the chemistry. Thus far, the Talent Catalyst has not interjected his or her own views and ideas into the Conversation. If the Catalyst had, she or he would be taking over control and responsibility for the participant before either understanding the participant's perspectives or giving the participant the opportunity to take charge on her or his own.

Step 3: Tap Your Success Stories

Does the success story need to relate directly to the participant's current issue?

No. The purpose here is to link concerns and successes. The Talent Catalyst invites the participant to look for patterns that have worked in the past. Some people try to jump from problem to solution. However, that's like flipping the switch on a pump and expecting water to gush forth. This step ensures that there is water in the pump (the participant's prior successes). Thus, instead of coughing and sputtering when it starts, the pump begins smoothly and successfully.

What if a success story doesn't come to mind for the participant?

Sometimes people feel so stymied by past problems that their storehouse of successes remains inaccessible. In this case, the Talent Catalyst could ask the participant if she or he would like the Talent Catalyst to offer one. Of course, the Talent Catalyst may not know the participant personally, so the story may be an inspiring account about someone else. Asking permission to provide input ensures that the participant retains responsibility and feels comfortable with the Talent Catalyst sharing.

What if the Talent Catalyst can't think of any relevant success stories, either?

No worries. The Talent Catalyst doesn't need to be a warehouse of wisdom. The Talent Catalyst and participant could take a few minutes to pick a success story from someone else or invent one. Alternatively, they could simply proceed to the next step. Although there is a certain order to the questions in the Talent Catalyst Conversation, the process is often nonlinear. The Talent Catalyst might say something like "That's OK. Let's move on to the next questions and see how they can help you." A great answer to the success story question might occur in the discussion about resources or putting together a team.

Round II: Expand Your Opportunities

Step 4: Identify Opportunities to Learn, Grow, and Develop

What kinds of learning, growth, and development are we talking about here?

It's important to inquire about not only the subject matter to be learned but also the changes in behavior and relationships accompanying the growth that a participant seeks. Often, it's a skill to be developed, like listening, or an inner shift, some inner quality that a participant needs to develop further. After all, with a few keystrokes, a participant can quickly find needed subject matter information on the Internet. Developing skills and boosting inner qualities such as curiosity or assertiveness can yield greater advantage.

Where can we find resources to explore topics like inner qualities?

Chapter 5 provides specific exercises to help you pursue this and other areas of growth and development.

Step 5: Use Your Resources

What if neither the participant nor the Talent Catalyst can think of particular resources?

If no resources come to mind, invite the participant to think about the resources that other people may have who are dealing with similar issues. Are there ways to access the kind of people, places, and things that those people have found useful?

How can the participant broaden awareness and development of relevant resources?

Check out the "100 Resource Challenge" in chapter 5, in the section "Your Resource Power-Up." It provides a structure to identify more resources and to use the resources more fully.

Step 6: Revisit Your Hopes

Why does this step have the participants revisit their hopes? Isn't this redundant because they expressed their hopes in step 1?

While the Talent Catalyst Conversation proceeds in a step-wise manner, it guides participants to explore and grow in the process. When participants first talk about their hopes, their hopes may be rather abstract or more about the direction they think they ought to pursue or what others have done. That's why this step helps not only to reenergize participants before they move into action but also to clarify what's important and, therefore, what actions will serve them best. Sometimes, participants even come to a deeper understanding about themselves and their situation that prompts them to shift their hopes.

How can a Talent Catalyst help the participant to reach a deeper level?

Listen for the participant's energy and interest. A Talent Catalyst can serve as a thermometer to measure what's hot for a participant. When you think you've heard the participant hit on a "hot" topic, reflect back what you hear. The Talent Catalyst's attention will help the participant to establish an even deeper foundation for action. Likewise, if the Talent Catalyst hears the words but doesn't sense the emotional and physical congruency with them, the Talent Catalyst reflects that to the participant.

Round III: Energize Yourself through Actions

Step 7: Make a Healthy Stretch

What if the participant can't think of a healthy stretch, and one doesn't come to mind for the Talent Catalyst?

Remember, the Talent Catalyst isn't the answer person. It's perfectly fine for the Talent Catalyst to ask, "How might the success story you shared with me and the opportunities you noted come together to offer a chance for you to stretch?"

Participants frequently focus on the obstacles and lose track of how they could access what's right in front of them and what has already worked for them. The Talent Catalyst can bring these strands together and precipitate new possibilities.

Keep in mind that for some people a healthy stretch may mean taking a leap forward, while for others it might mean pulling back from an unhealthy situation and taking better care of themselves.

The first sections of chapter 6 offer further guidance on how to frame and pursue rewarding stretches.

How does the Talent Catalyst navigate the fine line between being supportive and pushing?

The Talent Catalyst has a critical role of supporting the participant's hopes and the truth about the situation. The Catalyst doesn't tell the participant what to do or press for one choice over another.

Has the participant demonstrated readiness to stretch but not acknowledged it? The Talent Catalyst can invite the participant to contemplate living her or his hopes now. What might that look like?

An effective Talent Catalyst maintains a fine balance of supporting the participant in taking action without getting too personally involved in the process. If the participant remains in charge of her or his choices and appears engaged and energized, the Talent Catalyst has hit the right balance. If the participant demonstrates resistance, or if it's only the Talent Catalyst who wants to see the participant take a particular action, the Talent Catalyst has stepped over the line.

Step 8: Enlist a Talent Fulfillment Team for Results

What if the participant doesn't know some of the people who would be ideal?

Don't let the "how" block your identification of the "who." Talent Fulfillment Teams have power. The teams can lift participants up when they are discouraged and open doors and opportunities to help participants realize their hopes.

Research results indicate that people in the United States typically can connect with fewer than six friendship links. If they optimize the connection paths, the degrees of separation diminish to approximately three.[1] Existing members of a participant's Talent Fulfillment Team can help reduce the number of links needed and facilitate connections.

Would they agree to help?

When participants express and share their deepest hopes, other people feel a strong attraction toward helping them. See the section "Enlist Your Talent Fulfillment Team" in chapter 6 for stories and examples of ways to secure your star players.

Step 9: Target Concrete Actions

What's the right amount and timing of actions?

Even if the first action that the participant mentions sounds like a winner, the Talent Catalyst encourages him or her to consider additional possibilities. Choices give people a sense of power. Also, choices keep people from getting stuck pursuing something that looked good but doesn't prove fruitful. The Talent Catalyst confirms with the participant that the participant has a workable set of actions.

Step 10: Reflect on Your Possibilities and Progress

What's reasonable to expect from the Conversation?

Most Conversations have major, lasting impacts. When participants engage their constructive thinking to uncover their hopes, identify opportunities, and take actions, they overcome obstacles and move forward. The Conversations are truly catalytic and precipitate immediate actions and near-term results.

What if no major breakthroughs occur during a Talent Catalyst Conversation? Does it mean that the participant and Talent Catalyst didn't do a good job together?

No. Sometimes a Talent Catalyst Conversation plants seeds that take time to sprout. They may not germinate during the Conversation itself. We've had Conversations in which it wasn't clear during the Conversation whether the Conversation would have lasting value for the participant. Strikingly, we often hear later from such participants about new job responsibilities, better working relationships, and deeper fulfillment that they have experienced. How much of those results can be attributed to the Talent Catalyst Conversations and how much resulted from other factors? Again, the Talent Catalyst Conversations have the effect of activating reactions and results. They rely on the participants' accessing the resources and opportunities. Therefore, some participants need to let the roots take hold before solutions grow.

SAMPLE TALENT CATALYST CONVERSATION AND SUMMARY

Would you like to get some additional insights into a Talent Catalyst Conversation? This resource lets you sit in on an entire Talent Catalyst Conversation. We hope that "seeing one" will help give you the confidence to go ahead and "do one" as participant or Talent Catalyst, as well as some additional skills and insights that will support you in "teaching one" to someone else.

The following dialogue is an adaptation of a real Conversation and relates to Fran, one of the inspiring people featured in the book. You'll see how she powered up her talent story and moved into action. In addition, you'll see some commentary boxes that give additional insights into the process for both the participant (Fran) and the Talent Catalyst (Gary).

Fran's story is representative and inspirational. Still, it's important to remember that no two Talent Conversations are exactly alike. Some Conversations flow beautifully and lead people to absolute clarity and immediate action. Others seem to go in fits and starts until important openings occur. Yet others leave people in a place of contemplation rather than assertive action. We find that it works best to trust yourself and the process to come to just the right result for now.

THE BACKDROP

The following Conversation is set at a *Take Charge of Your Talent* workshop in a midsized service business. All of the managers and professional staff—from front-line supervisors to the CEO—attended the initial workshop, in which the Talent Catalyst Conversation was a centerpiece. The 150 attendees wanted to learn more about a fresh approach to talent development and the idea of being Catalysts for one another. The business had suffered some cutbacks at the outset of the recession and was looking for a better way to engage the untapped talent inside the organization.

THE PARTICIPANT: FRAN

We met Fran at the workshop. An effective senior analyst in the auditing department, Fran wanted to become a manager. Without prior experience in managing people, she didn't have the credentials required of applicants for supervisory roles.

THE TALENT CATALYST: GARY

In this illustration, the Talent Catalyst is Gary. Gary had prior experience watching a Conversation. He also had engaged in a Conversation directly as a participant and in another as a Talent Catalyst for a colleague. Thus, he appreciated both roles in the Conversation. With that experience under his belt, he was willing to move to the next level and demonstrate how to be a Talent Catalyst for someone else—in this case, lots of other people.

Fran and Gary volunteered to demonstrate a Talent Catalyst Conversation in front of the large workshop crowd so that the audience could see a Conversation in action. After their demonstration of each round, the audience members paired up to do the round on their own.

THE CONVERSATION BEGINS

While the crowd looked on, Fran and Gary briefly introduced themselves to each other. Each of them had a copy of the Talent Catalyst Conversation Guide, containing open-ended questions divided into three rounds: hopes, opportunities, and actions. The Talent Catalyst Conversation Guide includes an introduction to each round and some background for each of the ten steps in the Conversation. We've put the introductory and background information that they would read during the Conversation into sans serif text so that you can focus on their dialogue. You'll read occasional commentary from the authors, which is set out in boxes.

GARY: Good morning, Fran. Nice to meet you officially. I really don't know how much help I'll be able to be, but I promise that I'll do my best.

FRAN: Thanks so much for trying. Taking charge of my talent really struck a chord with me, so I am eager to try this Talent Catalyst Conversation. But I must admit that I feel a little self-conscious at the front of the room.

GARY: Hey, you're brave. But don't worry, we're all in this together, and I've been through it already. It's painless! Is there anything you want me to know before we follow the materials in the Talent Catalyst Conversation Guide?

FRAN: Well, I've been working in the organization for over ten years. I've always been in a staff role. Right now, for example, I'm a senior analyst in the auditing department. Oh, yes, and a year and a half ago I began an evening master's degree program.

GARY: OK. What would you like the focus of this Talent Catalyst Conversation to be?

FRAN: I'm really eager to see how I can advance in my career.

Opening Commentary

When you are a Talent Catalyst, remember to listen to the participant's responses and reflect back to the participant what you hear. Take notes as you go, so that the participant can just relax and be present. Keep in check any impulses to give advice or tell the participant what you think ought to be done. Participants need to take charge of their own talent.

Round I: Enliven Your Hopes

This round helps the participant to focus on what's important, consider concerns, and build confidence in the prospects for success. In short, it initiates the participant's constructive thinking to tap the creativity and motivation to move forward.

Step 1: Connect with Your Hopes

You need energy to make positive changes in your life. When you connect with your deepest hopes (that is, your interests and aspirations about the topic you've chosen), the energy you produce will help you to see possibilities and opportunities around you with more clarity. You will be more likely to make sound, creative choices that lead to better use of your talents; greater personal satisfaction; and more powerful contributions to your family, community, team, and organization.

GARY: What are your hopes about your work?

FRAN: I'd like to move up in the organization. In fact, I'd really like to take on more responsibility as a manager and leader.

GARY: OK, what I hear you saying is that you hope to advance and especially want to be supervising people. Why are these hopes important to you?

FRAN: I enjoy helping people and making a difference in what I do. It's all tied up in continuing to learn, building relationships, and getting meaningful results. I'm a people person. Of course, I work with lots of people, but I think I would feel more engaged with my job if there were leadership, teaching, and training components. At this juncture, I'd really like to be guiding others in their work and helping them to succeed.

GARY: So, you are enthusiastic about the prospect of guiding other people, and it's about more than just moving up the organizational ladder. It sounds like you're passionate about helping others to succeed.

FRAN: Exactly.

Commentary

Notice that Gary doesn't have to repeat each word Fran says. He just needs to reflect the essence of what she says. At this point, he can tell he is on the right track because Fran tells him so. If he had not reflected her accurately, she easily could have corrected him. This process of reflection and checking in keeps the Conversation on track.

GARY: Ready for step 2?

FRAN: OK, ready.

Step 2: Consider Your Concerns

When we focus on our deepest hopes, our brains often attempt to protect us from harm by generating stories of concern. Ignoring them could be dangerous; yet assuming they can't be overcome will also limit what is possible. For now, we suggest that you simply acknowledge their presence.

GARY: What's standing between you and realizing your hopes?

FRAN: The big obstacle for me is that I haven't had formal responsibility for supervising other people. I've volunteered to lead projects across departments, and those have gone well. But I haven't been responsible for direct supervision of employees. It's a chicken-and-egg dilemma. Most of the openings for supervisory positions I see ask that applicants already have experience in supervising other people. So it seems that I just can't get there from here.

GARY: Tell me more. Like, what would count as supervisory experience?

FRAN: Well, I know one requirement is being able to show that I can give effective performance feedback and do performance reviews. That's what I hear from managers, and I know that from my own experience as a staffer. I need to exhibit leadership qualities. And, of course, I'd need to have some understanding about the work of the department in which I'd be a supervisor.

GARY: Which of your concerns seems most important to address now so that you can make progress toward your hopes?

FRAN: I think it's the performance feedback piece that needs the most attention. It's where I feel least able to demonstrate my abilities.

Step 3: Tap Your Success Stories

We can look to the past to see how we have successfully dealt with similar concerns. Retrieving memories of past successes can provide clues to overcoming current issues, situations, or concerns.

GARY: How have you successfully dealt with concerns like these before?

FRAN: I'm thinking about my decision to start my master's. For the longest time, I thought it would be impossible. I was totally overwhelmed by the idea of working and going to school. How could I do all the work for the degree and keep up with my job at the same time? My husband encouraged me, and so did a friend and colleague who works in the same industry but at a different firm. Both of them knew the responsibilities I was up against. My husband just kept telling me that I could do it, as long as I took it course by course. I had to take the work on in manageable chunks. And then my friend reminded me that everything I learned would be readily applicable at work and might even help me to advance. I listened to their advice, and I'm halfway through the program. I'm glad that I'm pursuing the opportunity.

GARY: You got past what you thought was an impossible obstacle, and it's working out. What did you learn from that situation that might help you now?

Commentary

At this point, Fran twisted up her arms and legs tightly, showing that she was shutting down a little and feeling defensive. Gary didn't leap in and try to fix it; he just listened patiently.

FRAN: I can say that I've pursued a big goal before by breaking down the task. I also figured out how to find ways to make what I'm learning useful for the company and what I do at work helpful for my learning. That way, my growth didn't conflict with my job.

GARY: You found ways to resolve the possible conflict between your work and your master's program.

FRAN: Yes—for example, I used a work situation as the topic for a school project. The professor liked the practical insights, and my supervisor read it and we talked about how to apply the recommendations on the job.

GARY: Sounds like you have success stories that can help you now.

FRAN: Yes—when you put it in that light, I do.

Round II: Expand Your Opportunities

While your success stories may provide some approaches that you can build upon, significant progress requires new growth and learning. This round focuses on growth and learning, as well as the resources and expanded hopes that will help you to develop your talent. Note that chapter 5 will help you explore these issues more deeply. For now, you are developing an outline that will focus further thinking and action.

Step 4: Identify Opportunities to Learn, Grow, and Develop

As you work toward realizing your hopes, you will have many opportunities to learn, grow, and develop. This growth may be in knowledge, skills, or inner qualities like curiosity, assertiveness, or compassion. This process is likely to be energizing and pleasurable, as it opens up fresh possibilities to express your talent more fully.

GARY: How will you need to grow, and what will you need to learn to address your concerns and realize your hopes?

FRAN: I'll definitely need to learn more about best practices for giving people performance feedback. That's clear. I also see that I'll need to step out of my comfort zone in terms of asking for help and opportunities.

GARY: All right, let me see if I am getting this. You want to acquire some subject matter knowledge. And it sounds like asking for help is going to be kind of tough for you.

FRAN: Yes, I think I need to be more assertive if I want to be a manager. But I'm really feeling ready for that growth. I'll just need some practice to boost my confidence, especially if I supervise people who have been my peers.

GARY: I see. You want to show more confidence. You want to grow into a supervisory role, and you want to be able to successfully navigate the change in relationships that it will entail.

FRAN: That's it—that, and having the persistence to work through even the stuff that makes me uneasy.

Step 5: Use Your Resources

Resources feed our hopes. Everything we accomplish, we accomplish by using our resources: the people, places, and things that surround us and the capabilities within us. Often, concerns arise because we worry that we lack the resources to realize our hopes: "I hope to do X, but I don't have enough of Y (time, money, connections, ideas, education, skill, space, etc.)." When we recognize the abundance of our resources, our brains respond with a sense of possibility. We are emotionally, energetically, and creatively in a great place to move into our future.

GARY: What resources do you have that can help you to realize your hopes, Fran?

FRAN: When you say "resources," you are talking about money or time or what?

GARY: When I got this question in my Conversation, I went right to the financial part. But, yeah, "resources" means anything, anyplace, and anyone that can help you on your road.

FRAN: Let me see. In terms of people, there are the two that I mentioned before—my husband and my friend and colleague, who's actually been giving me informal advice. I also have a professor in my master's program who is a human resources expert. He might be a good resource. In addition, the young professionals group I joined has helped me to build relationships with managers at different businesses here in our area.

GARY: That sounds like a good start. Anything else? How about places or things?

FRAN: For places, I have the university for my master's program. And if an office counts, a manager offered to let me shadow him in his office for a few hours a week so that I could get a feel for a manager's work and literally see what things look like from that vantage point.

GARY: How about inner qualities you might use?

FRAN: I feel good about my interpersonal skills—and my managers have pointed out my ability to work well with people as an asset in my performance reviews. I love to learn, and I like to teach, too. I also speak enough Spanish to communicate the basics. But those really aren't inner qualities. I think assertiveness is the most important inner quality for me to work on.

GARY: Looks like you have a lot of resources you can draw on.

FRAN: You know, I think you are right. It seems like so much more when I talk about it.

Step 6: Revisit Your Hopes

Time to check back in with your hopes. Remember, we suggested that when you connect with your deepest hopes, the energy you produce will help you to see possibilities and opportunities around you with more clarity. You may wish to revise your hopes, either by articulating them in a different way or by prioritizing differently.

GARY: Do you have some greater clarity about your hopes?

FRAN: Yes, I do. I feel that things are coming into sharper focus.

GARY: How would you express your hopes now?

FRAN: Well, I'm still interested in gaining a supervisory role and helping others to succeed. I'm also clear that I hope to become more assertive in the process. What's shifted is that I see more resources and clearer opportunities to pursue my hopes. So my hopes feel more achievable.

GARY: I hear that your direction remains the same. And I can hear in your voice that you have more energy and confidence about your prospects for getting there.

FRAN: Yes. And, you know, I think I can move even faster than I imagined. I am definitely blessed with plenty of resources and a network of people to support me. All I need to do is ask for help. That's really essential. I do believe that a senior leadership position could be on the horizon for me.

GARY: So, you have a bigger vision, and it feels as though leading in a broader role is now more clearly within your grasp.

FRAN: That's it.

Round III: Energize Yourself through Actions

It's time for action! However, before you launch off with the first idea that comes to mind, this round invites you to consider a healthy stretch you might like to make: an objective you can reach for that is challenging, without causing unproductive stress or pain. Then it proceeds to who can support you and the actions you'd like to take to get started.

Step 7: Make a Healthy Stretch

One path to engage your talents is to honestly and joyfully make a stretch. This approach loses its power if the participant undertakes a stretch out of obligation or duty. You don't need to know in advance how you would accomplish the stretch. After this Conversation, you can follow the guidance in chapter 6 to pursue your desired stretch successfully.

> GARY: What might a healthy stretch look like in your situation Fran?
>
> FRAN: I'm not sure.
>
> GARY: Shall I offer some thoughts?
>
> FRAN: Sure.
>
> GARY: Is there a way that you could begin to do what you want right now? Maybe you could find an opportunity to get a real taste of the leadership role that you'd like or to lead a team in which you could provide the performance feedback that you need for your portfolio.
>
> FRAN: That would be great, if I had the chance. Frankly, I feel ready to jump into a supervisor position, but I don't see how to make something like that happen.
>
> GARY: I hear that you feel ready and need a chance. From what you've said, it sounds as if there may be some possibilities for you.
>
> FRAN: I suppose, but I'm not sure. What do you see?
>
> GARY: You mentioned that you have led projects across departments, and those have gone well. Is there a way you could demonstrate your performance feedback skills by giving people performance feedback on such projects?

FRAN: You mean just start doing what I want to be doing? Sure, I'd like that, but it may take a while for such projects to arise.

GARY: That may be so. But would you consider letting people know that you feel ready now to supervise others and would like opportunities to demonstrate that?

FRAN: That could work. It feels a little pushy.

GARY: Pushy or assertive?

FRAN: OK, you got me. Yes, assertive. I'd need to think about who would be the right people to talk with about moving forward.

GARY: OK. Let's see.

Commentary

At this point, the Talent Catalyst can link back to the responses from previous steps. Whether the participant chooses to make a healthy stretch, and what that stretch might be, is entirely up to the participant. It's not the role of the Talent Catalyst to tell the participant what to do or make the participant feel that there's a stretch that he or she "ought" to take. Gary was a skilled Talent Catalyst because he could listen between the lines and hold Fran's hopes for her. However, if you are the participant, make sure that the suggestions of your Catalyst line up with your own outlook and approach. In the end, the direction you decide to take is up to you.

FRAN: That does feel right to me. I'd like to try it.

Step 8: Enlist a Talent Fulfillment Team for Results

Imagine that you have a Talent Fulfillment Team of people who can support and inspire you. The world is full of people who can bring out your best and fill in your gaps of knowledge, skill, experience, and expertise. These can be people already in your circle and others beyond it. Think as big as you'd like. Later you can use the "Enlist Your Talent Fulfillment Team" section in chapter 6 for guidance on how to reach and engage the people you seek.

GARY: Who would be ideal to have on your team?

FRAN: A team just for me? All right, I'm going to think big. While I know that I need my manager and our department head to help me with my actions, I'd like to have the CEO of our organization, Tom, on my team. He seems genuinely interested in how people can advance in our organization. He invited me once to brainstorm with him for ideas, so I'm going to take him up on it. Another good person would be my friend who is an executive at another company. I really respect her as an advisor, and I expect that she could help me to see my situation from another perspective. I'd feel comfortable confiding in her and getting candid advice. Then there is the chair of my master's program, the one in HR. He'd be a good subject matter expert. I definitely also want my family to be supportive of my dream. The actions I've listed will take some extra time and effort outside the regular workday. I need my husband and kids to be on board; otherwise, I won't be able to do this.

GARY: You've mentioned people whom you already know. Is there someone you don't know well who may be able to help you "play big" to take action?

FRAN: Let's see. Thinking really big? I could get some ideas from the executive coach that our CEO has. The people I know who have worked with her always talk about her insights, and she has excellent connections too. Maybe once our CEO is on my team, he could introduce me. You know, speaking of CEOs, there are some female CEOs in our region who inspire me. I might network through women's leadership groups to meet them at conferences or other gatherings. Am I stretching too far?

GARY: Seems like you have a concrete list. I'm writing down the people for your team so that you can remember to enlist the ones you already know and network to meet the ones you don't.

FRAN: That sounds great. Thank you!

GARY: No thanks needed; they are all your ideas! Can you visualize these people cheering for you as you fulfill your hopes?

FRAN: It feels a little unreal, but I'd be ecstatic. I can see myself leading with confidence, and I can almost hear my team cheering for me.

Step 9: Target Concrete Actions

Critical to any success is taking appropriate, concrete actions. Take some small actions or make a big leap. Either way, act!

GARY: What forward-moving actions would you like to take now toward realizing your hopes?

FRAN: I'm feeling a little overwhelmed by the idea of launching into action. But I'm thinking about small steps. I could start with checking out opportunities to do a research paper for my master's program on best practices for performance feedback. Then, I could take that information and talk with my manager about my interests and how this work would be useful to me and the organization.

GARY: You've identified several actions to learn about performance feedback and build your skills in ways that also will benefit your organization. I notice that those pick up on the success story you shared earlier.

FRAN: Yes, they are manageable chunks that I can do to get going. And to embrace the challenge of starting to act like a supervisor, I will let my manager and special project teams know that I want to position myself to give performance feedback in real-life settings.

GARY: I am hearing that you plan to build your knowledge and skills and start applying them.

FRAN: Exactly. I don't need to wait to get the position I want. I want to start now to explore and enjoy the role of helping others to succeed with constructive performance feedback. But—and this is a big "but"—I need to take the work one step at a time so that I don't get overwhelmed. When I get overwhelmed, I just shut down. I was afraid a minute ago that I wouldn't be able to finish this Conversation.

GARY: Before we go to the next step, can I ask you what helped you to get over the mental hump and keep going?

FRAN: Besides the fact that we have 150 coworkers watching us? Seriously speaking, I went back to the image of my team, and I pictured my husband and my executive friend telling me to keep going with manageable steps. It's as if, just by imagining it, I felt supported. That relaxed me, and I got the idea to write the research paper.

GARY: Perhaps you can come back to that method as you take actions toward realizing your hopes. Do you feel that you have a workable set of actions for now, or is there something else you want to do?

FRAN: Well, I can see that I'll need to expand my network and get more people helping me to look for opportunities to apply my skills. I have plenty to get going.

Step 10: Reflect on Your Possibilities and Progress

Take a few minutes to digest the experience you've just had. As participants explore these questions with thoughtful Talent Catalysts, they often gain insights and identify opportunities and actions in the Conversation itself. For other participants, the Conversations create ripples that may require more time to demonstrate their effects.

GARY: And now, the final question for 100 bonus points. Just kidding—there are no points, but the Guide does direct me to ask, what have you gained from this Conversation?

FRAN: I believe that I'll get out of the impossible situation where I've felt stuck. I feel energized and ready to roll.

GARY: What will help you to follow through on your intentions?

FRAN: Well, I was wondering if I might check in with you in two weeks to report on my actions.

GARY: Sure. I'd be delighted to hear about your progress and encourage your efforts to get a strong start.

* * *

We caught up with Fran in a few weeks. The first thing we noticed was that she was wearing brighter colors. She seemed more confident. We had a very different impression of her from that of the shy woman we saw take a seat on stage just a few weeks earlier. She told us that she was ready to make some changes and that the Talent Catalyst Conversation had given her the boost she needed to get into action. Then she showed us the summary notes she was using from her Conversation with Gary.

GARY'S NOTES FROM FRAN'S TALENT CATALYST CONVERSATION

Summary of Round I: Enliven Your Hopes

1. Hopes

Advance to a supervisory role on a track to senior leadership.

Continue to learn and build relationships.

Help others to succeed.

2. Concerns

How to demonstrate proficiency in giving effective feedback and performance reviews (critical skills necessary to supervise others).

3. Success Stories

Started what seemed like the impossible task of an evening master's program while working full time. Learned to break it into manageable pieces and integrate school projects with day-to-day work.

Summary of Round II: Expand Your Opportunities

4. Opportunities

Learn more about performance feedback.

Develop assertiveness in asking for help in achieving goals; evolve from being a coworker to being a supervisor.

5. Resources

PEOPLE

Friend/female executive for informal advice.

Expert in human resources from master's program.

Networking program connections.

The young professionals group.

A manager who offered to let her shadow him in his office.

Female leadership group (for networking).

PLACES
Master's degree program.

Her office.

THINGS/INNER QUALITIES
Interpersonal skills.

Love of learning.

Love of teaching.

Basic conversational Spanish.

6. Hopes Revisited

Bigger vision of leadership opportunities and ideas to pursue them starting now.

Continue to learn and build relationships.

Help others to succeed.

Summary of Round III: Energize Yourself through Actions

7. Healthy Stretch

Begin now to behave like a supervisor by taking opportunities to give constructive performance feedback.

8. Talent Fulfillment Team

CEO of organization.

Senior female executive in outside organization.

Chair of master's program specializing in human resources.

Family to share the dream.

CEO's executive coach.

Female CEOs in the region.

9. Actions

Check out opportunities to do research paper on best practices.

Talk with manager about how this would be useful professionally and for the organization.

Connect with HR to gain support and opportunities.

Arrange to provide performance feedback for the team on special projects.

Let appropriate people know about wanting opportunities to supervise others.

10. Reflections on Possibilities and Progress

Sees a path around the obstacles to becoming a supervisor.

Following through on Talent Catalyst Conversation feels likely to increase use of talent and work satisfaction.

Plans to check in with Gary in two weeks to encourage accountability for a strong start.

SERVICES TO SUPPORT YOU

Take Charge of Your Talent is a global initiative designed to support a world where all people have the keys to take charge of their talent, and they enjoy using those keys to benefit themselves and others.

To deepen the opportunities and support available for you and to accelerate the global initiative, we offer the services described briefly below. For more information, visit www .TakeChargeofYourTalent.com, or send an e-mail to requests@ TakeChargeofYourTalent.com.

FOR INDIVIDUALS

You can deepen your experience with the Take Charge of Your Talent program with a Certified Talent Catalyst.

Certified Talent Catalysts

A Certified Talent Catalyst has specialized training to guide you through a Talent Catalyst Conversation and support your efforts to accelerate through obstacles and multiply the payoffs for yourself and others.

FOR ORGANIZATIONS

Stimulate a take-charge talent culture in your organization. The authors and Certified Take Charge of Your Talent Trainers and Presenters customize and deliver services for organizations across the continents. The services easily scale to reach participants up, down, and across your organization cost-effectively.

Keynotes and Presentations

We provide speakers for meetings and conferences that spark lively conversations and concrete actions for each of you to take charge of your talent.

Workshops and Programs

We customize offerings for the needs of both commercial and non-profit organizations to support a take-charge talent culture in your organization and enduring results.

Take Charge of Your Talent Champions Training

As part of all organizational programs, we encourage a minimum of 10 percent of the participants gain additional training to serve as Take Charge of Your Talent organizational champions; people who stand for and support a thriving talent culture.

Take Charge of Your Talent Coaching

We provide master coaches for executives who want to build and sustain Take Charge of Your Talent cultures.

GLOBAL HEADQUARTERS

Take Charge of Your Talent
895 Napa Avenue, Suite A-5
Morro Bay, California 93442
(805) 772-4667
www.TakeChargeofYourTalent.com

VISIT THE ONLINE COMMUNITY

Website: www.TakeChargeof YourTalent.com

Visit the website for a wide range of information and resources for you and your organization. These include the following:

Get Started Checklist: Identify your needs and interests and get connected with appropriate resources.

Community: Receive helpful tips, links to latest information, and invitations to local gatherings, global teleconferences, webinars, etc.

Blog: Gain new insights and take advantage of opportunities to share your questions and what you are learning.

Videos: See the authors and other Certified Talent Catalysts share insights about the Take Charge process, view Talent Catalyst Conversations in action, and see commentaries from participants.

We look forward to your visit.

NOTES

FOREWORD

1. For more about Melissa Poe Hood's story, see *The Truth About Leadership: The No-Fads, Heart-of-the-Matter Facts You Need to Know*, by James M. Kouzes and Barry Z. Posner (San Francisco: Jossey-Bass, 2010), 1–14.

INTRODUCTION: THE PERFECT MOMENT IS NOW

1. Since 1996, we have asked over 1,000 employed up-and-comers, senior managers, and members of teams and organizations two questions: (1) How well is your work tapping your talent that is relevant for your job? (2) How satisfied are you with your work situation? Whether they worked in profitable high-tech companies or high-performing local government agencies, respondents on average reported self-assessments in the 60 to 70 percent range for both questions. Within an organization and across organizational settings, there is a strong correlation between individuals' responses to the two questions. People who use more of their talent have correspondingly higher levels of work satisfaction.

2. Daniel H. Pink, *Drive: The Surprising Truth about What Motivates Us* (New York: Penguin, 2009), 62.

3. Margaret J. Wheatley, *Leadership and the New Science: Learning about Organization from an Orderly Universe* (San Francisco: Berrett-Koehler Publishers, 2006), 14.

4. Nikki Blacksmith and Jim Harter, "Majority of American Workers Not Engaged in Their Jobs," October 28, 2011, Gallup, Inc., http://www.gallup.com/poll/150383/majority-american-workers-not-engaged-jobs.aspx (accessed July 26, 2012).

5. Gallup Consulting, "Calculating the Cost of Actively Disengaged Employees," June 6, 2011.

6. Gallup Consulting, "State of the American Workplace: 2008–2010: How American employees have fared during one of the most challenging periods in the country's economic history." Chart on page 4 illustrates that the percentage "not engaged" or "actively disengaged" has varied narrowly between 70 and 74 percent for the decade 2000–2009. http://www.gallup.com/consulting/142724/state-american-workplace-2008-2010.aspx (accessed July 26, 2012).

7. Marco Nink, "Employee Disengagement Plagues Germany: Good workers and bad management crimp the country's productivity and GDP," *Gallup Business Journal*, reports for 2008 that 87 percent were "not engaged" or "actively disengaged" (varying between 84 and 88 percent over the period 2001–2008). http://businessjournal.gallup.com/content/117376/Employee-Disengagement-Plagues-Germany.aspx (accessed July 26, 2012).

8. Ashok Gopal, "Booming Singapore Sees Rise in Worker Engagement," January 4, 2005, Gallup, reports for 2004 that 91 percent were "not engaged" or "actively disengaged" (varying between 91 and 96 percent over the period 2001–2004). http://www.gallup.com/poll/14524/Booming-Singapore-Sees-Rise-Worker-Engagement.aspx (accessed July 26, 2012).

CHAPTER 3: CONNECT WITH A CATALYST

1. Reflective listening is a technique attributed to the work of Carl Rogers. Carl Rogers, *The Carl Rogers Reader* (New York: Mariner, 1989) and *A Way of Being* (New York: Mariner, 1995).

2. Daniel Goleman, *The Brain and Emotional Intelligence: New Insights* (Northampton, MA: More Than Sound, 2011), locations 642–43 (Kindle).

CHAPTER 4: KEEP YOUR HOPES HUMMING

1. David Rock describes the neuroscience underpinnings affecting thought patterns in *Your Brain at Work: Strategies for Overcoming Distraction, Regaining Focus, and Working Smarter All Day Long* (New York: HarperCollins, 2009), 108.

2. Shawn Achor reports on studies that support the finding that we perform better when in a positive state of mind in *The Happiness Advantage: The Seven Principles of Positive Psychology That Fuel Success and Performance at Work* (New York: Crown Publishing, 2010), 14.

3. W. Timothy Gallwey uses the formula "Performance = Potential – Interference" in *The Inner Game of Work* (New York: Random House, 2000), 17.

4. Robert Hargrove makes the distinction between "rut" and "river" stories in *Masterful Coaching* (San Francisco: Jossey-Bass, 2008), 125–29.

CHAPTER 5: GRAB OPPORTUNITIES TO GROW

1. Carol S. Dweck describes the theory and research for understanding the fixed versus growth approaches to life in *Mindset: The New Psychology of Success* (New York: Ballantine, 2006), 15.

CHAPTER 6: CHALLENGE YOURSELF TO STRETCH

1. Dr. Carol Scott, an emergency physician, writes about stress; its physical and emotional components; and the best stress zone for health, wellness, and performance in *Optimal Stress: Living in Your Best Stress Zone* (Hoboken, NJ: John Wiley & Sons, 2010), 244.

2. Jennifer Robison, "Disengagement Can Be Really Depressing," *Gallup Business Journal*, 2012, http://businessjournal.gallup.com/content/127100/disengagement-really-depressing.aspx (accessed July 26, 2012).

CHAPTER 7: CREATE ENDURING CAREER ASSETS

1. Susan Wloszczyna, "Paul Newman: A rare breed," *USA Today*, September 27, 2008, http://www.usatoday.com/life/people/2008-09-27-newman-obit_N.htm (accessed July 15, 2012).

2. Walter Landor (1913–1995) was a brand design expert and pioneer of branding and consumer research techniques. "A brand is a promise that creates a preference" is attributed to him on multiple websites. See, for example, the Branding 3.0 blog, April 29, 2010, http://marketplace insightscomportfolio.files.wordpress.com/2010/04/branding-blog-branding-three-point-o.pdf.

CHAPTER 8: SHARE THE WEALTH AND EVERYONE WINS

1. Jim Collins, *Good to Great: Why Some Companies Make the Leap ... and Others Don't* (New York: HarperCollins, 2001), 139.

2. Luke 4:24, *English Standard Version Bible* (Wheaton, IL: Crossway Bibles, 2001).

3. Terry Moore, "How to Tie Your Shoes," TED Talk filmed February 2005, posted May 2011, http://www.ted.com/talks/terry_moore_how_to_tie_your_shoes.html (accessed June 1, 2012).

CHAPTER 9: CHAMPION A TAKE-CHARGE TALENT CULTURE

1. Gallup Consulting, "Calculating the Cost of Actively Disengaged Employees," June 6, 2011, cited in introduction notes, estimates the US workforce aged 18 or older to be 134 million; Nikki Blacksmith and Jim Harter, "Majority of American Workers Not Engaged in Their Jobs," October 28, 2011, Gallup, Inc., cited in introduction notes, report 71 percent as "not engaged" or "actively disengaged."

2. International Labour Organization, "Global Employment Trends 2012: Preventing a deeper jobs crisis," 9, http://www.ilo.org/wcmsp5/groups/public/---dgreports/---dcomm/---publ/documents/publication/wcms_171571.pdf (accessed July 26, 2012).

3. Celent Communications, "Online Brokerages: Trends and Developments," February 5, 2009. Report estimated the number of online brokerage accounts in the United States at thirty to forty million. http://www.celent.com/reports/online-brokerages-trends-and-developments (accessed July 17, 2012).

FREQUENTLY ASKED QUESTIONS ABOUT THE TALENT CATALYST CONVERSATION

1. Much has been written, both scholarly and popular, on this topic. A classic study appeared in J. Travers and S. Milgram, "An Experimental Study of the Small World Problem," *Sociometry* 32, no. 4 (1969).

ACKNOWLEDGMENTS

We have so many people and organizations to thank for their insights, encouragement, and support in the creation of this book. First and foremost, we thank our families, Liz and Kate and Susan and Max, for their steadfast love and sacrifices of family time. We've also enjoyed the inspiration of many teachers, including Thomas Leonard, an early founder of professional coaching who challenged us to figure out how to train people to develop the essence of coaching skills within thirty minutes. That challenge prompted us to create the Talent Catalyst Conversation model. Shirley Anderson and many other leaders have supported us and our efforts from the beginning.

Professional colleagues and friends generously contributed insights for our efforts. In particular, we note John Steinhart, who originally recruited Don to the Stanford Graduate School of Business, and Professor Michael Ray, who taught the Creativity in Business course that Don attended in its first offering. They have been outstanding sources of wisdom, treasured friends, and powerful "Hope Holders" for our endeavor. Meg Wheatley also took an early interest in the project and, along with Michael Ray, recommended the book to Steve Piersanti, president of Berrett-Koehler. While we had heard wonderful reports about this publisher for years, we have been amazed and delighted by the kindly rigor of Berrett-Koehler's editorial, marketing, and production teams. They immediately understood and championed the vision of providing keys for everyone to take charge of their talent. We deeply appreciate Jim Kouzes's interest in the book and the insights and energy he brought to writing the foreword.

Suzanne Murray and Lauren Courcy Villagran provided very talented editorial assistance for the draft manuscript. Dorothy Kolomeisky served as our key editor. Her fresh perspective, creative ideas, animated language, and constant support arrived just when we needed them most.

Many clients in organizations large and small, for profit and nonprofit, have participated in workshops and Talent Catalyst Conversations and shared invaluable feedback. Frank Benest, who is a past president of California City Managers, a former city manager of Palo Alto, and now senior advisor to the International City-County Management Association, stimulated our early work to create a program that scales easily to serve people throughout an organization. We also appreciate Jim Collins's encouragement to think big about the impact that *Take Charge of Your Talent* could have. The *Take Charge* 20/20 Vision (twenty million people in twenty countries using the keys by the year 2020) arose from his concept of a long-term BHAG (big hairy audacious goal).

The success of the vision will require attracting many people from around the globe to share leadership of the endeavor. We are grateful to an early band of master coaches who provided suggestions for implementing the program. They include Siobhan Murphy (self-appointed and much appreciated "minister" for the effort), Andrew Cassidy, Gail Ginder, and Julia Fabris McBride. More recently, Heide Marie Klein, Axel Meierhofer, and others have offered interest, ideas, and leadership.

To all of you and many more people who continue to inspire, encourage, and support us, we express our deepest thanks.

INDEX

ABOUT THE AUTHORS

Don Maruska

As a founder and CEO of three Silicon Valley companies, venture investor, and recipient of the National Innovators Award, Don writes from a broad base of experience. His lifelong passions for creativity, translating innovative ideas into practical applications, and bringing out the best in others stimulate his work.

Don's own story is one of learning how to take charge of his talent. He was the first in his family's history to attend college, and he earned a BA magna cum laude from Harvard University. At twenty-two, Don was a legislative assistant in the US Senate and thereafter developed management procedures to implement a national housing program. He subsequently earned an MBA and JD from Stanford University and joined McKinsey & Company, where he led strategy and organization projects for corporations, government agencies, and nonprofits.

Following nearly two decades in Silicon Valley, Don became a Master Certified Coach, focusing on helping leaders and teams to cultivate success in their organizations. He is proud to claim that coauthor Jay Perry was one of his mentor coaches in learning the coaching profession. Don's clients include large firms such as Accenture, Blue Shield, Duke Energy, Intel, Microsoft, and Wells Fargo, as well as growing midsized businesses, government agencies, and nonprofits. He also founded and directs the Cal-ICMA Coaching Program, which provides professional development for over three thousand leaders in local government each year.

For more than a decade, Don wrote the "Business Success" column distributed through the Knight-Ridder Business Wire to more than two hundred newspapers in the United States and via Reuters overseas. He also wrote *How Great Decisions Get Made: 10 Easy Steps for Reaching Agreement on Even the Toughest Issues,* with a foreword by Margaret J. Wheatley. This book, reprinted in Asia and Africa, has helped businesses, governments, and communities around the world to enjoy major breakthroughs and enduring results. Don has appeared on over thirty radio and television interview programs throughout the United States. He delivers keynote speeches and workshops across the country and abroad.

Don and his family live on the shores of Morro Bay, California, where he enjoys the rhythms of nature amid thriving farming, fishing, and artist communities. As an avid swimmer and tennis player, Don is grateful for the lessons he learns from improving his skills.

Jay Perry

Jay Perry is a Master Certified Coach who helps people to take advantage of both business and personal challenges in unique and powerful ways. His clients include Fortune 500 corporate executives, entrepreneurs, and creative artists. He is also known as one of the world's leading mentors for new coaches seeking professional certification.

Jay's clients appreciate his fresh perspectives that help them to see themselves and their situations in a new light. He earned a BFA from Boston University and an MFA from Ohio University. With a background in professional theater as an actor, teacher, director, stage manager, and theater owner, Jay approaches his work with a sense of playfulness and a passion for developing creative communities. In the 1980s, he applied these skills in operating the Actors' Information Project to empower performing artists to take charge of their careers and lead healthy lives. He also served as CEO of a digital imaging and archiving business with offices in New York and Los Angeles.

Jay has coached and led workshops for thousands of people around the world on topics such as business planning, leadership, transformational change, coaching skills, communication, and career planning. In 1991, he began working with legendary coach Thomas Leonard and participated in the creation of Coach University and the International Coach Federation. Jay's coaching clients include executives at AT&T, Avaya, Genentech, GlaxoSmithKline, Shell, and Schlumberger. Additionally, he has a personal mission of bringing the benefits of coaching to traditionally underserved and at-risk populations and has volunteered his services in jails and prisons.

Jay lives in Charlottesville, Virginia, with his wife, Susan; dog, Mozart; and cat, Shadow. His son, Max, works in the entertainment industry.

Hopes

- more learning and growth
- affects a lot of people

Concerns

- organization, self doubt
- organization

Success Stories

- with action
- think positive, motivation
- If other can do it, I can do it too.

Opportunities

- learn more about job
- to set goals
- discipline, simplify

Berrett–Koehler
Publishers

Berrett-Koehler is an independent publisher dedicated to an ambitious mission: *Creating a World That Works for All*.

We believe that to truly create a better world, action is needed at all levels—individual, organizational, and societal. At the individual level, our publications help people align their lives with their values and with their aspirations for a better world. At the organizational level, our publications promote progressive leadership and management practices, socially responsible approaches to business, and humane and effective organizations. At the societal level, our publications advance social and economic justice, shared prosperity, sustainability, and new solutions to national and global issues.

A major theme of our publications is "Opening Up New Space." Berrett-Koehler titles challenge conventional thinking, introduce new ideas, and foster positive change. Their common quest is changing the underlying beliefs, mindsets, institutions, and structures that keep generating the same cycles of problems, no matter who our leaders are or what improvement programs we adopt.

We strive to practice what we preach—to operate our publishing company in line with the ideas in our books. At the core of our approach is stewardship, which we define as a deep sense of responsibility to administer the company for the benefit of all of our "stakeholder" groups: authors, customers, employees, investors, service providers, and the communities and environment around us.

We are grateful to the thousands of readers, authors, and other friends of the company who consider themselves to be part of the "BK Community." We hope that you, too, will join us in our mission.

A BK Life Book

This book is part of our BK Life series. BK Life books change people's lives. They help individuals improve their lives in ways that are beneficial for the families, organizations, communities, nations, and world in which they live and work. To find out more, visit **www.bk-life.com**.

Berrett–Koehler
Publishers

A community dedicated to creating
a world that works for all

Visit Our Website: www.bkconnection.com

Read book excerpts, see author videos and Internet movies, read
our authors' blogs, join discussion groups, download book apps, find
out about the BK Affiliate Network, browse subject-area libraries of
books, get special discounts, and more!

Subscribe to Our Free E-Newsletter, the *BK Communiqué*

Be the first to hear about new publications, special discount offers,
exclusive articles, news about bestsellers, and more! Get on the list
for our free e-newsletter by going to **www.bkconnection.com**.

Get Quantity Discounts

Berrett-Koehler books are available at quantity discounts for orders
of ten or more copies. Please call us toll-free at (800) 929-2929 or
email us at bkp.orders@aidcvt.com.

Join the BK Community

BKcommunity.com is a virtual meeting place where people from
around the world can engage with kindred spirits to create a world
that works for all. **BKcommunity.com** members may create their own
profiles, blog, start and participate in forums and discussion groups,
post photos and videos, answer surveys, announce and register for
upcoming events, and chat with others online in real time. Please join
the conversation!